Practical Guide to

HOME LIGHTING

by William F. Rooney

VNR VAN NOSTRAND REINHOLD COMPANY
New York Cincinnati Toronto London Melbourne

Practical Guide to HOME LIGHTING

Practical Guide to
HOME LIGHTING

A Van Nostrand Reinhold Book
published in association with
Hudson Publishing Company,
Library of Congress Catalog
Card Number 80-50367.
ISBN 0-442-22853-8.

Author: William F. Rooney

Executive Editor: Robert J. Dunn
Book Editors: Sandra L. Beggs
Sally Harms
Jane Williams
Copy Editor: Virginia Allen
Technical Consultant: William F. Rooney, Sr.
Art Director: Burt Sakai
Illustrations: Deborah Hopping
Graphics: Annette T. Yatovitz
Production Manager: Laurie Blackman
Composition: Wulf Schrader
Kathy Frederick

Cover Photography: John Fulker

Printed in the United States of America

Published by Van Nostrand Reinhold Company
A division of Litton Educational Publishing, Inc.
135 West 50th Street, New York, NY 10020,
U.S.A.

Van Nostrand Reinhold Limited
1410 Birchmount Road
Scarborough, Ontario M1P 2E7, Canada

Van Nostrand Reinhold Australia Pty. Ltd.
17 Queen Street
Mitcham, Victoria 3132, Australia

Van Nostrand Reinhold Company Limited
Molly Millers Lane
Wokingham, Berkshire, England

16 15 14 13 12 11 10 9 8 7 6 5 4 3 2 1

Table of Contents

Preface

Like beauty, good lighting is in the eye of the beholder. We take for granted the simple activity of opening a drape to let the sunshine stream into a room, or flicking a wall switch to turn night into day. We're surrounded by light, but know very little about it. And that's too bad, because when it comes to lighting, most of us are being cheated and we don't realize it.

As personal and important as it is, most of us have very little control over the lighting we live with on a day-to-day basis. In a new home, we leave the lighting decisions to the architect and builder. In an existing home, we have inherited the situation from the previous owners. When it comes to residential lighting, we probably don't even know what we are missing.

When discussing the subject of lighting with architects, most are knowledgeable about good practices for schools, offices, and stores. However, most admit that residential lighting is another question. "We never spent much time studying that in school." So, while designing a house, architects tend to specify minimum lighting standards without much individuality or imagination. And builders are even worse.

The typical builder usually follows the stock architectural plans. "Nobody ever complained about the lighting in my homes!" is as much a boast as an explanation. Too often, the homeowner does not even get the lighting that was originally specified. As his construction project nears completion, inevitably costs begin to exceed the budget. And since lighting is one of the last major items to be installed, "Well, we can always cut back there and save a few dollars," the builder explains.

At one time your local electric utility company offered a wealth of lighting assistance and ideas—kitchen and bath planning, recommendations for types of bulbs, fixtures, and minimum light levels for various rooms and tasks. But not today. Things have changed, and many utilities are no longer "promoting" increased electrical usage. Now their information activities are confined to weatherstripping, insulation, and a variety of other energy-saving programs.

If you shop for light fixtures on your own, you won't be overwhelmed with information. General merchandising stores usually have packaged fixtures on a shelf, and the clerk will be happy to read you the price off the box. Retail lighting stores may have a better selection and often provide massed wall or ceiling displays of various fixtures. Yet even here, you still have no real idea how an individual light fixture will perform in your home. Few sales people take the time to discover the size of your room, ceiling height, light level needed, and how your family uses the space during the day and in the evening.

If you want to improve your residential lighting, you will need some help. And that is what this book is all about. The aim is to provide a practical guide for home lighting. Basic concepts like what is light, how is it measured, and how does the eye see will be covered. Natural and artificial lighting is explored, with information on how best to select and use it in your home. Light levels for various work areas are defined, and a simple method for using your 35mm camera meter to measure existing light in each room is explained. The action of light and its interaction with color is explored. The partnership of light and color has possibilities few homemakers realize.

Additional chapters delve into light for decorating and drama, for safety and security, and for indoor plant growth. The book closes with information on lighting equipment, a glossary, and a list of supply sources so that you can translate your lighting ideas into action.

Lighting is a very personal subject. It is both creative and practical. Well-planned lighting is neither expensive nor complicated. In fact, a carefully planned program can be cost- and energy-efficient. With the help of this book, you can light up your life. It's an exciting, challenging adventure in expanded living.

Architects: Natkin & Weber, AIA
Photography: Joshua Freiwald

Using natural light in the home is an excellent way to cut your energy bills. The home shown here utilizes plenty of sunlight to heat and light its interior. Oak trees outdoors let in varying amounts of light, creating changing patterns in the interior spaces.

1 The Philosophy of Light

Artificial light is the one element that separated early man from all other animals. Unlike the animal that operated from sunup to sundown, light provided man with 24-hour control of his environment.

When primitive man discovered fire and firelight, he found more than release from the fear of darkness. When daylight waned, he was able to move easily in and around his cave or hut. He was warmed against the cold of night. Man felt secure from wild animals and other marauders. This release from the bonds of darkness provided man with the psychological benefits of artificial light. For the first time he had a safe environment in which to think, create, and express his artistic feelings, as witnessed by the early, colorful cave paintings.

From this breakthrough, supplied by a useful artificial light source, man's inventiveness produced many adaptations of the flickering fire. First came flaming wood torches, fueled by pitch and natural resins found in pine and other wood species. Torches were portable, for use while traveling or hunting at night. They became lighting fixtures when fastened to the wall of a cave or hut.

Next came oil lamps using animal or fish fats and oils with a bark or cloth wick. Many of the early stone and pottery oil lamps are displayed in museums around the world. This primitive light source has survived to this day in the form of oil, kerosene, or gasoline lamps and lanterns. Lively, flickering flames still hold a fascination for many modern homemakers, especially on social occasions. Portable lanterns are still useful to campers and sportsmen traveling into areas away from modern electric power lines.

Along with the advent of oil lamps came the development of tallow and beeswax tapers and candles. This turned out to be one of the most significant happenings in the history of residential lighting. Candles and tapers, functional as they are, proved to have an aesthetic appeal as well, with their slim lines, smooth surfaces, and attractive shapes. Lighted candles, set in beautifully designed holders and fixtures, have an attraction that years have not diminished. Even the most sophisticated modern hostess uses candles around the house at times, to establish an inviting atmosphere for special occasions—from a romantic candle-lit supper for two, to a festive grade-school birthday party complete with the candle-blowing ceremony. All indications are that candlelight is here to stay. And, too, candles are most welcome in an emergency when electricity suddenly fails.

In the 1800s and early 1900s, interior and exterior lighting from illuminating gas was supplied by gas utility companies. It was piped along streets and into residences and commercial buildings for general lighting use. Available at first were flickering gas flames that could be raised or lowered to provide the desired intensity of light from wall, ceiling, or exterior lanterns.

Later, gauze mantles were developed, which could be placed over the gas flame, providing a larger and brighter glowing light source. In spite of the "Gay Nineties" atmosphere, gas lighting was never really

Light comes in many shapes, colors, and sizes. The General Electric bulbs, shown above, can be used for general lighting, accent lighting, and special uses.

accepted in America. It did attract a few who were willing and able to try something new, but it could not compete with electric lighting, which came along before gas illumination could gain a foothold.

Incandescent Lamps

Electric light became a reality in 1879 with Thomas Edison's invention of the first practical electric *light bulb.* Encased in the clear glass bulb was a long-burning carbon filament that glowed brightly as the electric current was passed through it. The use of the new *incandescent lamp* spread rapidly as Edison and others quickly designed electric generating plants, street distribution systems, and interior wiring circuits, outlets, and controls.

Today, the descendants of Edison's first lamp are available in many sizes, shapes, and colors. They continue to be useful for general lighting, accent lighting, and special uses.

Fluorescent Tubes

In the 1930s, fluorescent tubes came into being, providing highly efficient *lines of light,* ranging in length from 6 inches to 8 feet. Later developments brought out circular, semicircular, and U-shaped fluorescent lamps. The availability of *white* fluorescent tubes, in various values of cool and warm tints, brought new emphasis to the partnership of light and color. Now, *mood lighting* can be achieved readily. For more pronounced color treatments, tubes come in various colored coatings.

What is Light?

To make the best use of the partnership of light, sight, and color, the character of each of the partners and their interrelationships must be totally understood.

Light is such a commonplace thing that we give little thought to its complex nature. Offhand, we are ready to accept the dictionary definition, which says: Light is that which makes it possible to see—opposed to darkness. A more technical definition gives us a better understanding of why light permits us to see: Light is a form of radiant energy that acts upon the retina of the eye, optic nerve, etc., making sight possible.

Radiant energy wave lengths are measured in nanometers (a billionth of a meter). The magnitude of radiant energy ranges from a low of a small

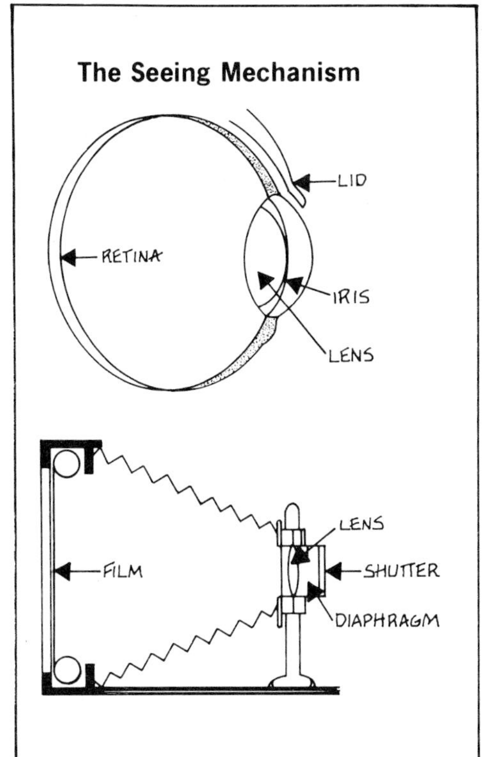

Fluorescent tubes, like the one shown above from General Electric, light up dark spots over a desk, in the attic, under kitchen cabinets, or over a workbench. This particular version has a woodgrain finish and a directional shade. It plugs in anywhere, is energy efficient, and lasts for years.

fraction of one nanometer for cosmic rays to more than 5,000 nanometers for electric power energy. In both natural and artificial light, radiant energy is found in the relatively narrow band known as the *visible spectrum,* between 375 and 760 nanometers. This spectrum band contains all the colors, which mixed together produce a *white light.*

A simple experiment will break up a narrow beam of light into its component colors. When the beam is passed through a transparent optical prism, we can see separate light bands colored violet, blue, green, yellow, orange, and red.

How We See

What we call sight is the act of seeing performed by our eyes. The human eye is a focusing and recording mechanism that has a close resemblance to a camera. The eye and the camera each have a lens, which focuses an inverted image on a light-sensitive surface—on the retina of the eye, and on the film in the camera. Fortunately, our brain turns the inverted retina image right-side-up, so the view recorded in the eye appears normal.

The eyelid corresponds to the camera shutter. When raised, it allows light wave lengths to enter and reach the retina. The iris in the eye performs the same function as the diaphragm of a camera. It opens or closes to regulate the amount of light entering the eye.

There is one important difference between the human eye and the camera. The eye is a living organ that automatically adapts itself to a great range of light levels. Also, without conscious effort on our part, our eyes automatically make the continuous changes necessary for good vision under changing conditions. A camera, by comparison, is a mechanical device whose parts cannot adapt to changing light or be harmed by such changes.

To be both useful and comfortable, light must be of the proper quality. The way, for instance, that a printed book page registers on the retina of an eye is very important. This demonstrates one factor about quality in lighting: the contrast between the amount of light falling on the book page and that falling on the immediate background. It can be expressed more exactly as: the relative brightness between the book page and its surroundings. This

Photography: General Electric

The setting above is the ideal light situation for reading. The light falling on the printed page is approximately three times that of the surrounding background. Any other light ratio is likely to tire the eye.

takes into consideration both the amount of light on the surfaces, and the amount reflected by the surfaces. A very bright page against very dim surroundings is a most uncomfortable and tiring situation. The opposite brightness contrast, a very dim page against a very bright background, makes the eye work hard to discern details on the book page.

The photo above illustrates a comfortable seeing situation—about three times as much effective light on the book page as on the surroundings. This type of lighting combination is an eye-saver and does not tire or strain the eyes over long periods.

Color and Color Perception

Color is the third partner, which can and should contribute to the design of an effective and satisfying home lighting system. White light, as we know, is composed of a mixture of the color wavelengths in the visible spectrum. This is one basic fact about color that should not be overlooked in the selection of colors in home decoration.

Another basic fact, often neglected, is that the apparent color of any surface is the color of light reflected toward the eye by that surface. For example, a stark white wall lighted by a pink light will no longer appear white, but will have a soft pink cast. A dead black wall will always appear black under any color light, since black is the absence of color—there are no colored pigments in the black surface to reflect any colors in the light by which it is illuminated.

The effect that two different colored light sources have on identical colored cards is shown in the picture of a two-compartment color booth on page 79 in Chapter 7. The left-hand booth is lighted by a daylight fluorescent lamp that has strong blue wave lengths. The right-hand booth is lighted by an incandescent lamp with amber characteristics. Both booths are illuminated to the same intensity.

This demonstration of an apparent color change, brought about by a change in the color of the light sources, shows the importance of careful coordination of light and color in developing a home decorating scheme. Fabric colors examined in a decorator's shop and paint colors considered in a paint store should be selected under the color tones of light to be provided in the area or room where the fabrics and paints

Photography: Harold Davis

The amount of light to be specified for each seeing task should be only one of the lighting factors. The kinds of light sources are also important. For example, the recessed fixtures in this kitchen may be more energy-saving than incandescent globe fixtures. The skylight helps plant growth and brightens the kitchen psychologically.

will be used.

The one element in our environment about which people have strong individual preferences is color. It is quite common for a woman to say, "Blue is my color," or "I like a red dress for a party." Men may not be as outspoken, but it is easy to guess that some businessmen constantly wear conservative blue and gray suits so customers and clients will consider them prudent managers.

Psychologists have found the reactions people have toward colors is quite universal within individual societies. Certain colors are associated with certain moods. Reds, oranges, and yellows are accepted as stimulating. These are considered warm colors. Blue, blue-violet, and violet are least exciting. They are cool colors. There is general agreement that warm colors appear to advance toward the eye and make space seem smaller, while cool colors recede and give a feeling of spaciousness. And everyone has a subconscious preference for sunlight or a white light source rich in red hues that provides "that healthy look."

Quality of Lighting

So far, the term *light* has designated the raw radiant energy given off by various light sources, which, if it reaches our eyes, will cause sight. The term *lighting* has a much broader connotation. It refers to the useful energy output of a system consisting of light sources, fixtures to support them in appropriate locations, wiring channels to activate the light sources, and convenient electrical controls. Such a system provides only the basic elements, yet too many people consider it to be "adequate lighting."

Today, the development of an efficient and satisfying home lighting system demands the consideration of many factors besides the basic ones just listed.

The amount of light to be specified for each kind of seeing task should be only one of the lighting factors. So much emphasis has been placed on the need for "adequate lighting" that many consider the amount of light on a work surface to be the way to measure the quality of light.

Take the case of the man whose struggle with income tax forms in his den on evenings was giving him eye strain. To conserve energy he used a desk lamp only, with all other lights in the room turned off. Although he

Photography: Westinghouse Electric

Photography: Harold Davis
Designer: Walter Dunivant, Interiors of Palm Desert

A controlled lighting effect for an entrance hall arrangement can be seen in the photo above. Fluorescent sources are concealed within a trough, and the light is refracted or redirected to enhance the grouping of paintings. Shallow picture frames are used to minimize shadows.

Venetian blinds or shutters, above left, are a reliable means of reducing sunlight's glare. They are more efficient at this task than shades or curtains because the glare can be modified rather than simply eliminated. The new styling of venetian blinds creates endless decorative possibilities, and wood shutters always enhance an interior.

had an adequate 70 footcandles of light on his desk top, he still had problems because he was not aware of complete lighting specifications.

For instance, the desk light should be positioned so that its intense beam would not be reflected into his eyes by the papers on which he was working. If he were a right-handed writer, the desk lamp should be on his left so that his hand would not cast shadows on his work papers. The shade on the desk light should be luminous to reduce the contrast with the lighting on his desk top.

For even more comfortable lighting, other lights in the room should be turned on to eliminate dark surroundings as he raised his eyes from his work. The intensity of such general lighting in the den should be approximately 15-20 footcandles for comfortable seeing.

Controlled Light

Raw light waves, given off by incandescent bulbs and fluorescent tubes, do not, in themselves, constitute high-quality lighting. Since they travel in straight lines, they are scattered equally in all directions whether needed there or not. The early lighting engineers, faced with this problem, found ways to redirect and modify such light rays for more efficient and comfortable lighting.

Metal hoods with white enamel or polished metal surfaces were placed over incandescent bulbs to capture and redirect light rays to areas to be lighted. The effect of polished metal surfaces was termed *specular reflection*. When the reflective surfaces were matte surfaces, they produced *diffused reflections*, scattering the light rays as they were being redirected.

The engineers learned that 100 percent of the light reaching a surface would not be reflected. The natures of different surfaces would account for varying percentages of light being absorbed by the surface. The term *reflectance* is defined as the ratio of the intensity of the light reflected by a surface to the amount of light falling on it. For example, a wall painted in a medium tone of brown might absorb 60 percent of the light falling on it, and reflect 40 percent, giving a 40 percent reflectance value.

Another method of light control is *transmission*. Light rays can be diffused by passing them through translucent materials such as glass,

GENERAL LIGHTING SUGGESTIONS

Living, bed, family or recreation rooms	Suspended or surface-mounted fixture wattage	Recessed fixture wattage	
Small (under 150 sq. ft.)	Three to five bulbs, total 150-200W	Incandescent: Fluorescent:	Four 75W or four R-20 50W* Two 40W
Average (185-250 sq. ft.)	Four to six bulbs, total 200-300W Two fixtures or more	Incandescent: Fluorescent:	Four 100W or five to eight 75W R-30 or 150W R-40* Four 40W
Large (over 250 sq. ft.)	1 watt per sq. ft. and 1 fixture per 125 sq. ft.	Incandescent: Fluorescent:	One 100W per 40 sq. ft. or one 75W R-30 per 40 sq. ft.* Two 40W or six 20W per 100 sq. ft.
Kitchen, laundry, workshop			
Small (under 75 sq. ft.)	150W incandescent or 22 & 32W circlines	Incandescent: Fluorescent:	Two 150W Two 40W
Average (75-120 sq. ft.)	150-200W incandescent or 22 & 32W to 80W fluorescent	Incandescent: Fluorescent:	Four 100W Two 40W
Large (over 120 sq. ft.)	Incandescent: 2 watts per sq. ft or Fluorescent: Approx. 1 watt per sq. ft.	Incandescent: Fluorescent:	One 100W per 30 sq. ft. Two 40W or six 20W per 60 sq. ft.

Actual light from individual fixtures depends on whether bulb is exposed or shaded, the type of shade, etc.
*R-20, R-30 & R-40 concentrate warmth. Should not be aimed directly at head of seated person.

Courtesy: Progress Lighting

plastic, paper, and fabrics. Examples of this method are parchment shades on table lamps, and plastic panels on fluorescent fixtures. Since some light is absorbed in transmission, the surface brightness of such shades and diffusing panels is lower than that of the bare light source.

Redirection of light rays is also possible by passing them through a lens-type transparent glass or plastic panel. The rays are *refracted* or bent to a specific angle needed for the specific lighting application. An example of the use of such refraction panels is to effectively light a wall mural or picture collection.

To provide the proper angular direction of light, refraction panel fixtures can be mounted on, or imbedded in, the ceiling.

Brightness and Glare

Brightness and glare are two lighting terms often confused. Brightness could be considered a positive term and glare a negative term. Both of these lighting conditions are determined by the same set of factors.

Brightness can be defined as the intensity of light on an object or surface that directly reaches the eyes of the viewer. The apparent brightness of an object or surface can vary, depending on such factors as the position of the viewer, the position of the light source, and the contrast of the surface with its background.

Glare, on the other hand, is any brightness that causes discomfort, and interference with vision or eye fatigue. A highly polished surface can cause uncomfortable brightness or glare. A matte surface, which diffuses the reflected light rays, may minimize the glare effect.

Uniform general illumination of a room, with no discernible brightness contrast, makes an uninteresting home interior. Careful attention to the reflectance values of objects in the room and of the background areas such as walls, ceiling, and floor will produce more interesting and attractive home settings.

In the following chapters, the light and lighting principles briefly outlined here will be developed and further explained as they are applied to specific home situations. Lighting is not really that complex, but an understanding of the basic factors will provide the background for the practical and creative lighting ideas to follow.

Today people are trying to conserve energy, and what better way than by using natural resources. As shown here, Wasco Skywindows make excellent use of natural light to make a sun porch a really sunny, bright place for plants and people.

2 Natural Light

Natural light is sunlight, that radiant energy arriving from the sun at "the speed of light," 186,282 miles per second. The sun, 93,000,000 miles from earth, is the central body of our solar system and the star around which the earth and other planets revolve.

The sun has an approximate diameter of 865,000 miles, about 109 times the diameter of the earth. It appears as the largest and brightest of the stars visible to the naked eye, but it is among the smallest and faintest in the universe. This contradiction arises from its comparative nearness — the next nearest star is approximately 300,000 times as far away. Some stars have diameters 800 times larger than that of our sun.

This relative smallness compared to other stars in no way diminishes the importance of the sun to our earth. Throughout history, light has been associated with happiness, safety, and well-being; darkness with fear, danger, and human misery.

In contrast to other sources of energy, daylight is our most abundant natural resource. The supply is inexhaustible, readily available, and, best of all, free. Sunlight has long been a prized asset. In early England glass windows were taxed as a luxury. In this country, the original settlers would remove the glass panes from their existing house and take them with them as they journeyed westward.

Today, as we learn more about the methods to take full advantage of this natural resource and as our society becomes more complex, sunlight takes on added importance. There is a growing body of law concerning itself with "air-rights." What legal protection does a property owner have in the space above his land? Can a neighbor arbitrarily block a view or interfere with the flow of natural sunlight?

Natural Light Limitations

With all its benefits, daylight is not constant. The illumination it provides varies with location, time of day, weather conditions, seasons, and adjacent surrounding objects. Since the earth revolves around the sun, the amount of light we receive depends upon the angle of the sun in the sky at different times of the day. Because the earth's axis tilts as it rotates around the sun, a second set of varying angles develops as the seasons change.

The intensity and color range of natural light constantly changes as the sun moves across the sky. Cool and shadowless before sunrise, the predawn light is low in intensity, and colors in the environment are barely distinguishable. Sunrise makes a dramatic change. The nearly horizontal light is warm as the sky brightens, and form and texture are revealed to the eye. At noon, the light direction is nearly vertical overhead. Shadows are then the blackest, colors their truest. The daylight at noon is closest to pure white. Later in the afternoon, the light begins to fade again and colors are warmer. By sunset in the evening, colors are reflected from the clouds, patterns of light and shadow grow less distinct, and night falls, canceling out the sun's generosity.

The amount of daylight available for interior illumination varies with

Photography: Ezra Stoller

Because light is constantly changing, it offers exciting decorative possibilities, which we can explore and enjoy with the design and placement of windows. The home shown above has interior spaces that are carefully designed to take advantage of natural light's decorative qualities.

weather conditions. The overcast sky provides a lower level of light, fairly uniform regardless of direction. Windows facing a clear sky will be brighter with stronger shadow contrast. A window facing away from direct bright sunlight may receive less illumination than another window would on an overcast day.

An additional and sometimes confusing factor when dealing with natural light is the reflective effect of surroundings. Sunlight striking and bouncing off the sky, water, and ground surfaces, as well as reflected from adjacent parts of the house all contribute in varying degrees to light received through skylights, patio doors, and windows.

While the sun does produce natural illumination, it also creates brightness, glare, and shadows, which must be compensated for in planning. Although daylight levels vary from place to place and from time to time, the factors are known. Today we are familiar also with the variables of room dimensions, skylight and window sizes, shades, drapes, and other control devices.

Capturing Natural Light

To capture and use natural sunlight to its best advantage requires careful planning. The architectural profession has been slow in recognizing the impact of both natural and artificial lighting in residential design, but fortunately things are changing. With the growing concern for energy conservation and a better understanding of lighting principles, commercial and residential design now works with and not against good lighting practices.

The acknowledged master of light design is Alvar Aalto, the Finnish architect. Although respected in design circles, his architecture does not rank with the buildings of Mies or LeCorbusier for visual drama and majesty, but, as a recent article in *Time* magazine stated, "No architect has ever succeeded more brilliantly in flooding his interiors with the sun's own radiance. Aalto's skylights and windows are dazzling in the way they are cut and angled to catch every single ray. He could fine-tune a space, with a burst of reflected overhead light or a network of soft rays crisscrossing each other on surrounding walls, as perfectly as Stokowski conducted an orchestra."

Good light design starts with placement of the house on the building

Photography: Wasco Products

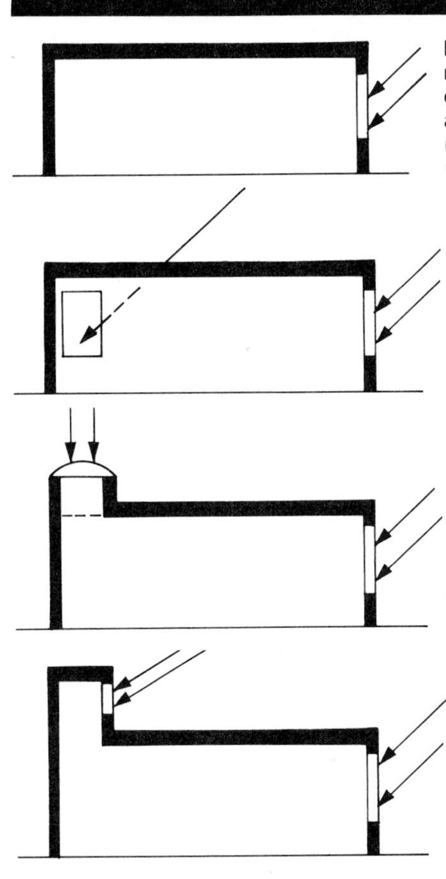

Lit from only one side, this room will be darker at the opposite end. Even though actual light levels at the rear may be high, the contrast will make the room seem gloomy.

Side lighting from a window at the rear will help balance illumination. (If lit from one end only, a practical room depth is 2½ times the height from floor to window head.)

A skylight at the opposite end of the room is another device that raises light levels in that space and brightens the rear wall to lighten contrasts.

Adding a clerestory window is another way to accomplish the same effect of reducing contrasts, though its light will vary more than a totally exposed skylight.

site. In colder climates, most of the glass may be on the southern and western exposures to soak up the sunlight. In warmer climates, however, the design may be modified or reversed to avoid the too-hot, too-bright summer sun. Homes in the north usually have relatively narrow roof overhangs so that the sun has full play on the building sides, while homes in the warmer climates need wide overhangs to protect the windows from direct sunlight glare.

In architecture, the rule of thumb is that rooms should be no more than 2½ times deeper than the height from the floor to the top of the window. Deeper rooms will appear gloomy since little light can reach from the windows to inside back wall surfaces. This restriction can be overcome if the design provides for additional light from side windows, skylights installed at the opposite end of the room from the windows, or the addition of a clerestory window along the center of the home to reduce the room light contrast.

Skylights

Although skylights have long been used on commercial and industrial building roofs, they are just becoming accepted for residential use in this country. Despite the psychological and aesthetic advantages of natural light through skylights, the previous abundance of low cost energy and the general unfamiliarity with the product has restricted its use. But energy is no longer a low-cost item, and the technological advances have greatly improved the skylight performance while lowering the cost. The skylight has finally arrived.

As a product, skylights are very effective and efficient lighting sources. The roof-mounted units are directly exposed to sky and sunlight. This horizontal illumination is two to five times the illumination on the average vertical or wall surface. This means that one square foot of skylight can provide as much light as five square feet of window surface.

Window light is restricted to the room periphery, while skylights can be placed to illuminate any interior space. For those homes that for some reason cannot be ideally situated on the building lot to maximize natural light, skylights may be the only efficient answer. Coming from overhead, the skylight illumination gives the same effect as electric lighting.

Above left, professional home builders and architects are beginning to recognize the advantages of working with, not against, the expanded use of natural light. Learning to flood an interior with radiant sun not only cuts down on energy bills, but also makes for a more pleasant place to live.
To maintain comfortable visual conditions at the rear of a room which has natural light from one side only, plan on a practical room depth about 2½ times the height from the floor to the window head. With depths greater than this, the difference in illumination levels near the window and at the rear will make the room appear gloomy. To give more even illumination throughout the room, top lighting and cross lighting from other directions will reduce shadows and glare. See diagrams above.

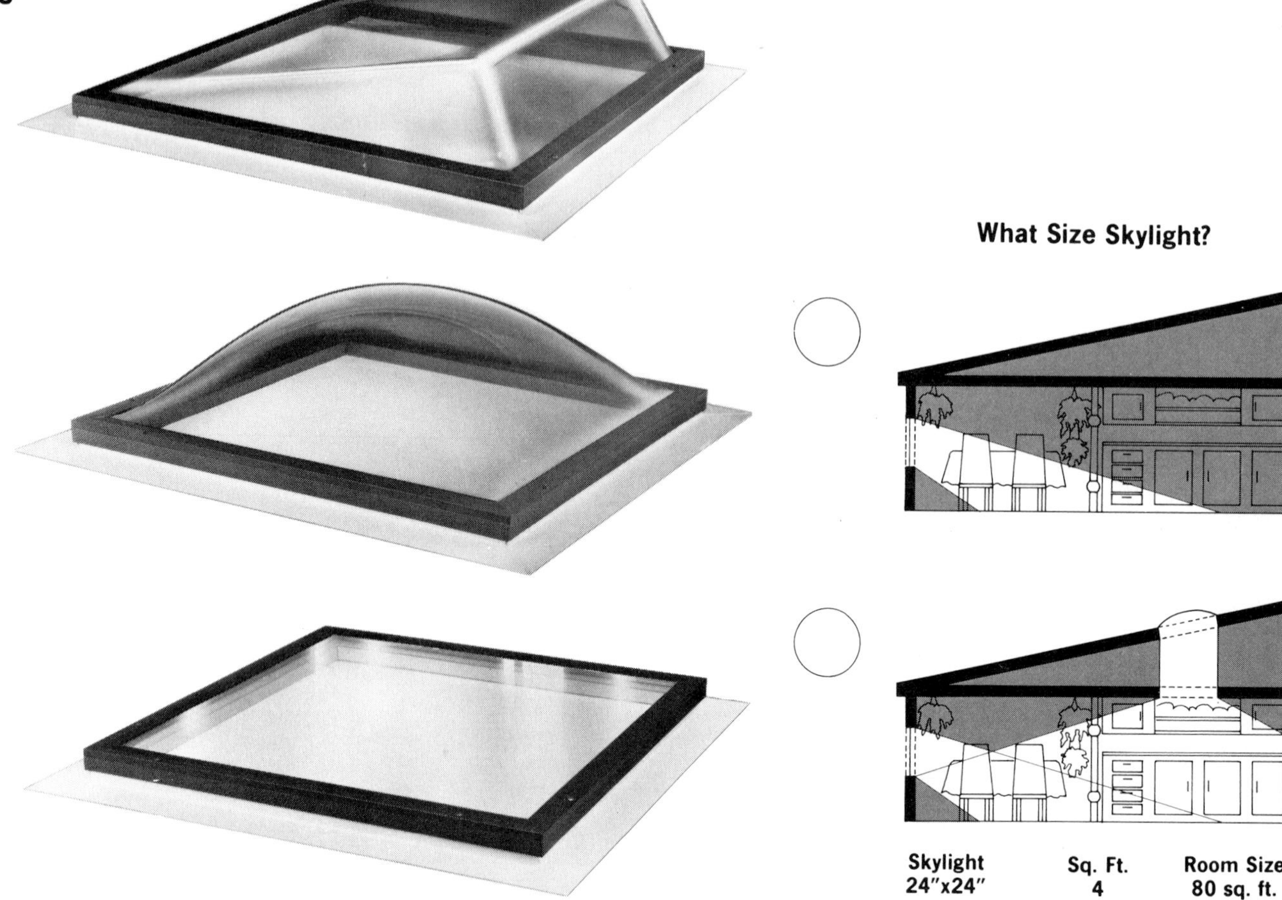

Above left, Wasco Products, Inc., has introduced a new line of skylights called Skywindows. The line includes the popular bubble or round window, a dormer-shaped window (both with thermalized, 100% acrylic double domes), and a double glazed Skywindow fashioned in flat safety glass.

The illustration on the right shows that the rafter spacing in your home is a major factor in determining the size of skylight to be used. Most houses have 16 or 24 inches, center to center, of rafter spacing. After finding out the correct rafter spacing in your house, it will be easier and more economical to install the proper skylight.

Shadows are not created as would be the case with window side lighting.

As a result of this efficiency, skylights covering 10 percent of the roof area are almost always sufficient for most general lighting needs. To determine the proper amount of skylight area, every square foot of skylight will accommodate about 20 square feet of floor. For instance, two 24" x 24" skylights (8 square feet) will provide general illumination for a 10' x 16' room (160 square feet).

Spacing between skylight units varies according to the height of the room. In high ceilings, units should be spaced approximately half a room height apart. For low ceilings, spacing can be 1½ times the room height.

Skylights are available in several different models. The most common is the curb-mounted skylight with an integral flashing configuration that simply caps down over the supporting curb. The curb, approximately 4 to 6 inches high, is built of wood, concrete, or metal, then secured and flashed in the standard roofing method. Curb skylights are used on flat or pitched roofs and are the most popular model.

Self-flashing skylights are designed to be installed directly into the plane of a pitched roof. They have a lower, cleaner profile than the curb style, but are not recommended for flat or shallow pitched roofs. The round or sun-bubble skylight is self-flashing and circular in shape. They may be installed on the roof or into a vertical wall surface and used as a window. The only drawback for wall use is the slight visual distortion due to the curvature of the plastic material.

In addition to the fixed skylights, operable models, which can be opened for ventilation, are available. The units open from the bottom slope about 10 inches. For windows too high on a ceiling to reach by hand, poles or long cords are provided. For an extra cost of from $150 to $200, automatic controls permit the skylight to open or close at the touch of a button.

When considering a skylight, three decisions must be made before your final selection. The size of the skylight width will largely depend on your roof rafter spacing. Most rafters are 16 or 24 inches center to center. Skylight widths are made to conform to these standard spacings. For example, if you have rafters on 16-inch centers, you can use a 16-inch skylight or one in multiples of 16

Photography: Wasco Products, Inc.

Photography: Owens-Corning Fiberglas Corp.

inches — 32 or 48 inches wide.

The second skylight decision concerns a single- or double-dome unit. If the skylight will be installed in a location where heat insulation and possible condensation are not major factors — garage, greenhouse, patio cover — then the single-dome unit is acceptable. However, in colder climates or where insulation and condensation may be a problem, the double-dome model is recommended. The dead air space between the two plastic layers creates a thermal insulation barrier without hindering the light transmission ability of the skylight.

The final question to be answered is skylight color. Clear plastic skylights give maximum light and visibility, but in some climates may be too hot or produce excessive glare. Translucent white plastic diffuses the light, providing even distribution without any harsh glare. Bronze-colored skylights also eliminate the glare, reduce heat transmission, and blend better with residential roofing materials.

Windows

With all the current talk about energy costs, heat loss, and temperature gain that overloads air conditioning systems, why don't we forget about windows, build with solid insulated walls, and rely on skylights and artificial interior lighting for our illumination? It's an interesting theory, but not completely sound, and it overlooks one critical factor — people. Windows can play a big part in a person's emotional health. Writing in the *Journal of the American Medical Association*, Dr. Samuel Vaisrub says walls represent visual prisons of enclosed spaces and that rooms without windows fail to provide an outlet for visual curiosity. He cites one study that showed that patients in windowless rooms were twice as likely to exhibit postoperative delirium. If all that sounds too scientific, just ask a real estate dealer how much extra a prospective buyer is willing to pay for a house with a panoramic view.

Today's windows, particularly the modern wood window, are a far cry from the rotting, paint-peeling, sticking, drafty window of the past. Now quality wood windows are factory-treated with preservatives to make them highly resistant to weather. The precision built parts and hardware are engineered to

The attic bedroom pictured above left makes use of natural light to illuminate it during the day. This greatly cuts down the use of electric lights and saves on energy costs for this homeowner. A pull-down shade covered in matching fabric shuts out the light when the occupant wants to take a nap.

Natural light from skylights can be utilized to brighten a bathroom interior as seen above right. The increasing use of day-lighting in contemporary architecture adds a decorative effect as well as cutting electricity costs.

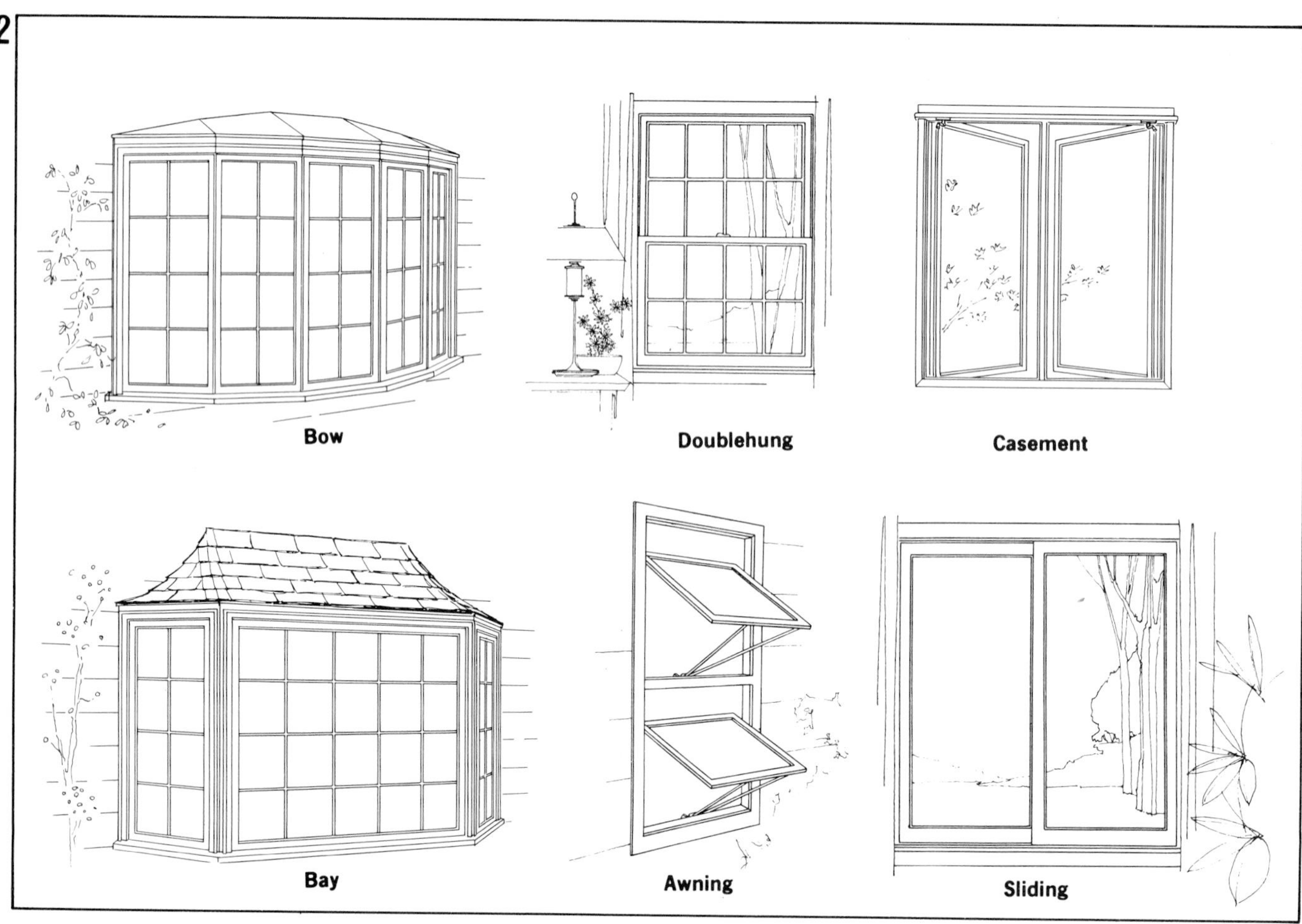

Windows are available in a number of designs, as shown above, to handle several specific applications.

operate without jamming or catching and open smoothly with little effort.

The natural insulating properties of wood are enhanced with factory-applied weatherstripping that keeps air infiltration to a minimum, reduces heat loss, keeps out dust, and reduces heating and air conditioning costs. The modern window is easier to wash. Many are designed to let you wash both sides of the window from inside the house.

The quality of natural light a window provides depends on its size, shape, and orientation toward the light source. A tall, vertical window will generally supply more light into a room than a long, horizontal design. Since the sun comes within normal viewing angles when it is low in the sky — from the east in the morning, from the west in late afternoon — east- and west-facing windows may be subject to glare. This can be minimized if the window can be placed high enough on the wall to avoid a direct view.

Windows are available in a number of designs engineered to handle specific applications. The *double-hung* window consists of two sash that slide up and down in channels in the window frame. This is the most popular style used in more than half the homes in the country. The sash on a *casement* window is hinged at the side and swings outward by means of a crank or lever. This is the most weathertight design and can be cleaned from within the home.

Sliding or *glider* windows have two sash that slide horizontally, right or left, in a common frame. These come in large sizes and provide a sweeping view. *Awning* windows are normally hinged to swing up and out. If they swing in and down, they are sometimes called *hopper* windows. This style is often stacked vertically or combined with other styles. *Bow* and *bay* windows are often added in remodeling since they can add living space to an existing room. The *bow* window unit curves out gracefully, while the bay window is straight in the center and angled at each end. Both designs can add either floor space if they are extended to the floor or sitting space as window seats.

The window design you select depends on the architectural styling of your home and which design functions best for your needs. The double-hung, bow, and bay windows are more popular for colonial and

Photography: Andersen Corp.

Environmental glazings with bronze and gray-tinted glass and coated reflective glass have been added to most of Andersen Corporation's top-of-the-line Perma-Shield windows. The energy-efficient environmental glazing options are effective in reducing solar heat gain and glare, which, in turn, helps cut utility costs.

traditional architecture. The casement, sliding, and awning styles are more modern and contemporary in feel. The double-hung is awkward to operate over a kitchen sink or counter. Here, a casement model can be cranked or levered open with one hand. If you have a walkway or patio immediately outside a window, the crank-out awning or casement may present a traffic problem. A double-hung or slider is more convenient for these locations. Sliding windows high on a wall provide light without sacrificing wall space for furniture.

When selecting windows, remember their style affects air flow for ventilation. Casement windows open 100 percent of their sash for complete ventilation. Double-hung and sliding windows provide 50 percent, awning style approximately 25 percent. In planning for natural lighting, don't overlook the added benefit of cross-ventilation cooling with your windows.

Modern Glazing Materials

Glass, of course, is the most common material used to glaze windows. In planning for natural light, you should be aware of the different types and treatments available today. The selection is a bit overwhelming.

The older type of window glass was called sheet glass. It gave a distorted view and is no longer popular today. The typical material now is *float* glass, 3/32 inch thick for single-strength and 1/8 inch thick for double-strength. *Plate* glass is actually float glass, thicker by 1/4 inch or more. This is the material often used in large residential windows, storefronts, or coffee-table tops.

Insulating glass, sometimes called *thermal* or *double* glass, is two pieces of glass with a dead air space between them. The space acts as insulation to reduce heat gain and loss. Some insulating glass has the two sheets bonded into the window frame, while another type actually heat-welds the two sheets into a thin hollow envelope.

Tempered glass is treated by a process of heating and cooling to make it three to five times stronger than untempered glass. In addition to its strength, when tempered glass does break, it crumbles into small safe pebbles rather than sharp splinters. For this reason building codes require tempered glass in shower, patio, and entrance doors.

Photography: Karl Riek

Controlling natural light can be achieved in a number of ways. Above, vertical blinds can be opened wide to let in maximum light or slightly closed to minimize light.

The effectiveness of your natural light source can be enhanced by intelligent use of reflected light. Where direct sunlight is not always available, it is often possible to "bounce" or reflect light into a window. As the reflectance chart, above right, indicates, light reflected from the sky off fresh snow or water loses little of its illumination power. Light surfaces outside a window will throw light into an interior.

Reflectance Values, Ground Surfaces

When lighting experts compute the illumination from the sky reflected onto the window from the ground, the following colors and textures of various ground surfaces must be taken into consideration:

Surface	Reflectance
Grass fields, lawns	6%
Bare earth	7%
Gravel	13%
Macadam	18%
Wild fields	25%
Concrete	55%
Old snow	64%
Fresh snow	74%

Wire glass has diamond-patterned wire mesh embedded within the glass as it is formed so that when broken, the wire tends to hold the glass particles together. This material is often used in skylights and as glazing in high crime areas. Another safety glass is *laminated* glass, which consists of two sheets sandwiched around a layer of clear or tinted plastic. When broken, the plastic layer holds the fragments together. The lamination is a safety feature, but also provides weather protection and theft security if the glass is broken. The lamination has one additional benefit — sound control. Tests conducted at airports with identical sound meters placed inside and outside the glass indicate a 90 percent decibel decrease in relative loudness within the room. As housing density increases along with highway and air traffic, the sound control properties of laminated glass will become more important.

Other specialty glasses include *patterned* glass where rollers create textures, ribbing, and decorative surface effects. *Reflective* glass has a mirrorlike coating of transparent metallic oxide baked onto the surface of plate glass to reflect up to 70 percent of the sun's heat and cut light transmission by up to 50 percent. *Heat-absorbing* glass is available in green, gray, and bronze colors with varying degrees of opaqueness to absorb solar heat.

To the various types of glass you can add a new generation of plastic glazing materials to expand your selection. Tough, weather-resistant acrylic plastic sheets have replaced the more expensive tempered glass for some safety applications. It is now available in the traditional clear, a variety of transparent colors, and a number of decorative surface textures. The plastic is flexible enough to be bent into arches or cast into bubble windows.

When you take the various window designs and combine them with the variety of single-, double-, and even triple- glazing techniques using the float, tempered, and other specialty glasses and plastics, there is a selection to meet any natural light situation. In fact, one major window manufacturer offers 1,062 different window and glazing options.

Controlling Natural Light

Often the quality of natural light is more important than the quantity.

Light Reflectance
Paint and Wood Tones

Color	% Reflection
Whites:	
Dull or flat white	75-90
Light tones:	
Cream, eggshell	79
Pale pink, pale yellow	75-80
Ivory	75
Light green, blue, orchid	70-75
Light beige, pale gray	70
Soft pink, light peach	69
Medium Tones:	
Pink	64
Apricot	56-62
Tan, yellow-gold	55
Yellow-green	45
Light grays	35-50
Medium turquoise	44
Medium light blue	42
Old gold, pumpkin	34
Rose	29
Deep Tones:	
Cocoa brown, mauve	24
Medium green and blue	21
Medium gray	20
Dark Tones:	
Dark brown, dark gray	10-15
Olive green	12
Dark blue, blue-green	5-10
Forest green	7
Natural Wood Tones:	
Birch, beech	35-50
Light maple, light oak	25-35
Dark oak, cherry	10-15
Black walnut, mahogany	5-15

Natural light entering a room through a skylight or window can be amplified and re-directed from within the interior. Light-colored walls and ceilings help spread the illumination. While an all-white room with white rugs is both dramatic and light-efficient, it may be impractical for a family with schoolchildren and pets. Use the chart above to work out the best compromise between light and livability with various paint and woodtone reflectance values on ceilings, walls, and floors.

You can always add light through artificial means where necessary, but controlling the intensity of natural light can be a problem. Glare or too-bright light can be controlled from either outside or inside the home. However, if excessive heat transfer is part of the problem, it is wiser to reduce the heat before it strikes the window. Sometimes it is as easy as using a sound landscape plan. Evergreen trees placed between the sun and your windows will filter both glare and heat year round. In cooler climates, deciduous or leaf-bearing trees will provide summer shade, and when the leaves fall in the autumn, winter sun filters through supplying both light and some warmth.

A new home can be designed with a broad roof overhang to block the vertical summer sun, yet allow the more horizontal winter sun to penetrate to the windows. For existing homes, outside sun shades, trellises, fiberglass patio covers, or roll-up bamboo shades can be used as light- and heat-control items. The new solar screens do more than keep the bugs and flies out. They are constructed like miniature venetian blinds that give good visibility, allow light and cooling breezes to penetrate, yet block off the direct rays of the sun.

Existing homes can also take advantage of the new tinted sheet film applied to windows to reduce both glare and heat. The sun control films, available in silver, bronze, smoke, and gold tints, can be easily applied by the homeowner. Some reduce up to 75 percent of the sun's heat, 82 percent of the visible light, and 98 percent of the fabric-fading ultraviolet light.

Inside the home, sun control and reflectorized window films can be applied to the interior glass surfaces. These coatings, together with insulated double-glass and storm windows, prevent heat loss to the exterior during colder winter months. Louvers, venetian blinds, and heavy drapes, some with reflectorized linings, can give the homeowner flexible control of natural light during different times of the day or for various seasonal conditions.

One of the simplest ways to maximize natural light in a room is also the cheapest. Wash the windows and keep them clean. It's as basic as that. Dirty windows can reduce illumination as much as 40 percent.

Photography: Bill Hedrich, Hedrich-Blessing

There are many decorative elements in this living/dining room that benefit from artificial lighting. The ceiling-mounted track lighting keeps the double-story living room from appearing cavernous. The art collection also requires dramatic track lighting.

3 Artificial Light

A comparison of natural and artificial light brings out several basic differences. Sunlight, light from the sky, and to a lesser degree moonlight—those natural light sources—are constantly changing in intensity and color quality. They can be modified only by mechanical means—by drapes, curtains, blinds, treated glass, or surface reflection. Most of these changes are negative, reducing the amount of light reaching your home.

Artificial light, by contrast, is a very flexible medium of illumination. We have fingertip control of intensity by switches and dimmers, and color quality control by interchanging bulbs and tubes. There is a broad variety of incandescent lamps, fluorescent tubes, and specialty light sources available for any application or location in your home. Most of these light sources produce *raw light.* These light rays should be redirected or modified in various ways to provide efficient and comfortable visibility conditions or desired decorating effects.

Incandescent Lamps

Since they are descendants of Edison's first carbon filament lamp, incandescent lamps are known to lighting engineers as *filament lamps.* Most of us, however, generally call them *light bulbs.*

The light bulb is a simple device with four main components: a glass bulb, a metal screw base, a tungsten filament, and an inert gas enclosed in the bulb to inhibit disintegration of the filament. The inside-frosted bulb is the most common home light source. The inside frosting diffuses the light rays given off by the glowing filament with only a 2 percent loss in light output. Since the outside of the glass remains smooth, the bulbs are easy to keep clean.

The size of the bulb is expressed in *watts*—the amount of electricity it consumes, i.e., a 60-watt bulb. The size is also indicated by listing the outside diameter of the bulb in ⅛s of an inch. A 60-watt A-shaped bulb that is 2⅜ inches in diameter is listed as an A-19 size. The size designation is important when buying decorative type bulbs that will be used bare, without a shade. The light output is given in *lumens,* which in the case of a 60-watt, inside-frosted bulb is 870 lumens. Also significant is the operating life of the bulb expressed as the *average life in hours.* For the same 60-watt bulb, the life figure is 1,000 hours.

A-shaped, inside-frosted bulbs are truly "household bulbs" for general use. They fill the sockets in table, desk, and floor lamps and in lighting fixtures of many types. The operating characteristics of the widely used type of light source are:

Watts	Size	Initial Lumens	Average Life-Hrs.
25	A-19	235	2500
40	A-19	455	1500
60	A-19	870	1000
75	A-19	1190	750
100	A-21	1750	750
150	A-21	2880	750
200	A-23	4010	750

The differences in the operating life for the various sizes of bulbs need some explanation. Incandescent lamp designers constantly strive to

Illustration Source: General Electric

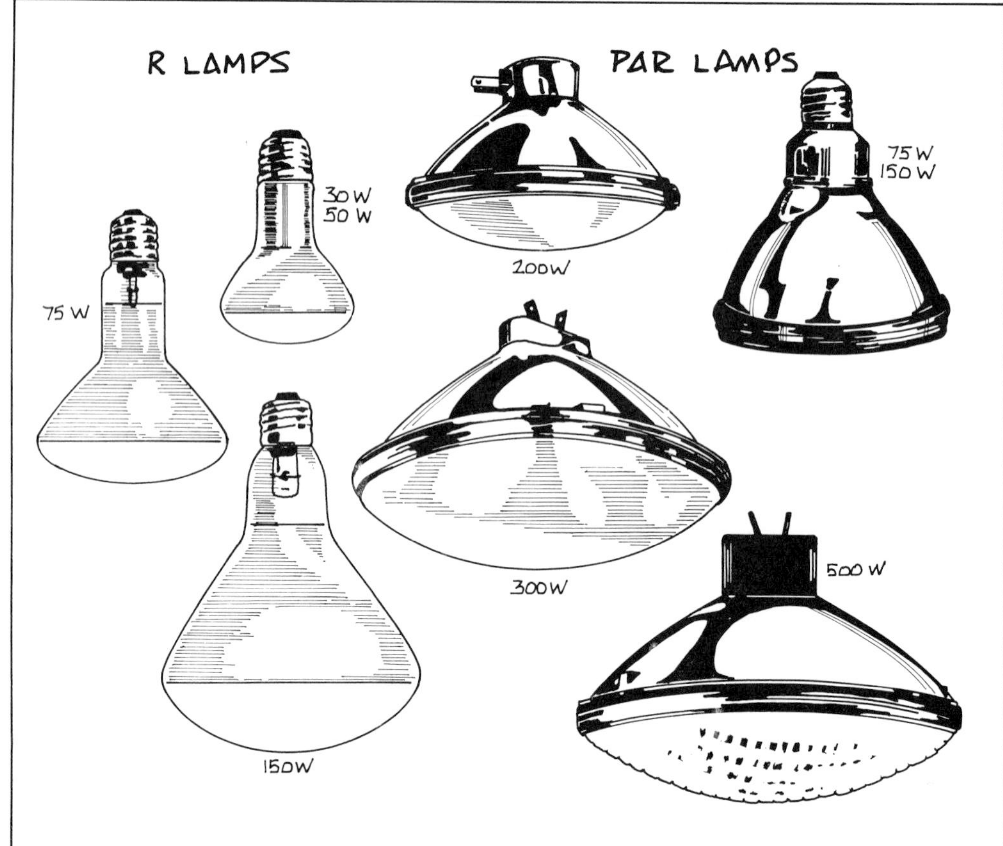

Illustration Source: GTE Sylvania

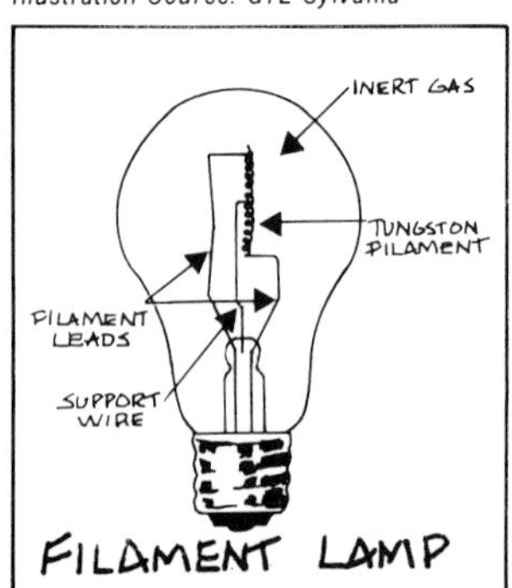

The illustration above left shows a filament lamp, known as the common light bulb. From 1879 until 1938 the incandescent lamp was the single source of residential electric lighting. Thomas Edison used a piece of charred bamboo as his bulb's light source. Tungsten is the modern filament material used.

The montage above right shows a mixture of reflector lamps and projector lamps. Reflector bulbs, known as "R" lamps," are mold blown of soft or hard glass. Their inner surface is coated with vaporized silver, which has higher reflectance than aluminum. The lamps are available in spot and flood beam spreads.

Projector bulbs are also called PAR lamps — parabolic aluminum reflector lamps. They are made of hard heat-resistant glass that is pressed into two molds, one for the reflector portion of the lamp, the other for the lens. Their manufacturing precision gives PAR lamps a higher degree of beam control than R lamps.

improve the efficiency of the light source, which is expressed in lumens per watt. The cost of using the bulb over its normal life is calculated, then the engineers strike a balance between the economics of use and the efficiency of output. The values given in the previous table have been determined from years of experience. They are the operating specifications that will assure the most light at the lowest cost.

A variety of A-shaped bulbs, known as 3-way bulbs, provide flexible intensities of light for many styles of lamps. These require special sockets and switches. Common household sizes of 3-way bulbs are: 30-, 70-, 100-watt, 50-, 100-, and 250-watt. Low intensities supply relaxed conversational light levels or, at the turn of a switch, higher, stronger light for close work.

Since the original frosted bulbs were introduced, new, slightly heavier "frostings" have been developed that achieve a maximum diffusion of light from the filament without glare or harsh shadows. These are *soft white* or *eye-saving* bulbs.

The concern with energy conservation has resulted in the introduction of long-life household bulbs. One manufacturer calls them *Super Bulbs*. Life of the lamps has been doubled, sacrificing about 12 percent of the light output. Such long-life bulbs are especially convenient for stairwells and other equally hard-to-reach locations.

Reflector lamps are directional light sources with built-in reflectors providing either a concentrated beam or spread beam. These lamps are available in two types of glass bulbs. The *R* bulb is made of soft glass for indoor use, with the neck and sides of the bulb coated inside with vaporized aluminum or silver to form a reflector. For general lighting, clear glass bulbs are often imbedded in the ceiling. Most sizes are available in spot or spread beams. Common household sizes are 30, 50, 75, 100, and 150 watts. The 75- and 150-watt sizes also come with bulbs in a variety of colors.

The second type of reflector lamp is known as the *PAR lamp* (parabolic aluminized reflector). These bulbs are made of hard, heat-resistant glass that will withstand outside weather conditions. Since the lens portion is made of pressed glass, the bulbs come with various beam spreads, from a very narrow slot to a wide floor

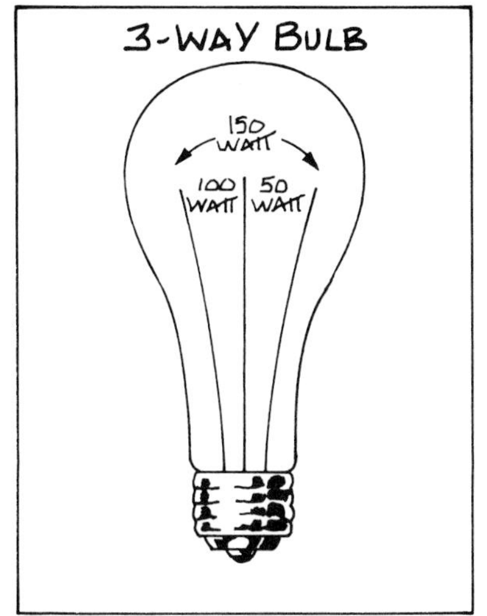

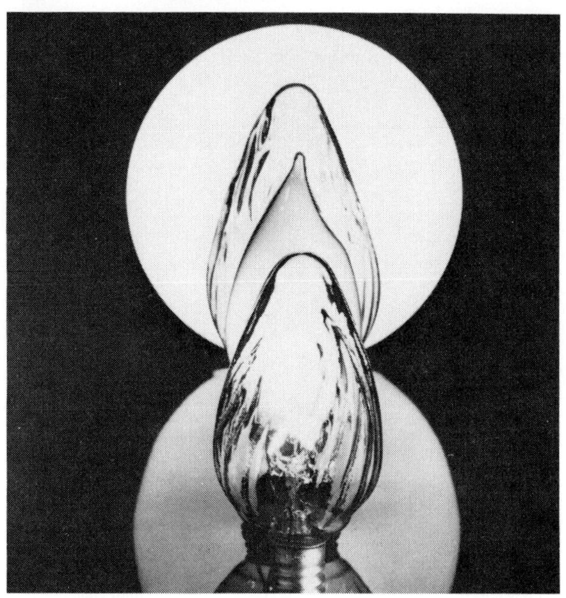

The cross-section of a three-way bulb, above left, shows the schematic arrangement of the two filaments. Each can be operated separately or in combination with the other. First the low-wattage filament is switched on separately, then the two together to give three lighting effects.

Tubular lamps of small diameter, see photo upper right, are generally known as showcase lamps. They fit easily into niches and other tight spaces or into reflectors mounted on picture frames, as shown here, available from Brookstone.

A new series of long-life, flame-shaped bulbs from Sylvania, lower right, can help reduce costly bulb replacement. The series includes units with rated lives of up to 4,000 hours. Also, they are especially useful for hard-to-reach fixtures like chandeliers.

of light. For home lighting, 75- or 150-watt sizes are recommended. Both sizes come with a clear glass lens. The 150-watt size, however, is made also with a variety of color lenses. These are used quite often to produce unusual landscape or other surface effects.

PAR bulbs (pear, straight neck) are general service lamps that are essentially elongated A-shapes. Two types in the 150- and 200-watt sizes are adaptable for home lighting. White bowl lamps have a translucent white coating on the inside of the bowl. This coating reduces both direct and reflected glare from open fixtures. The reflector type *silver bowl* lamps in 150- and 200-watt sizes are designed for base-up burning. Light is redirected toward the ceiling to provide general indirect lighting.

Tubular lamps of small diameter are known generally as *showcase lamps.* They fit easily into niches and other tight spaces or into reflectors mounted on picture frames. Popular screw base types are available in tube diameters of 1 1/4 inches (*T-10),* in lengths from 6 to 12 inches, and from 15 to 75 watts in capacity. This tubular bulb also comes with built-in silvered reflectors.

Lumiline lamps have the filaments extending the length of the lamp for a continuous line of light. This type of tube light has a disc base and requires a special socket. Standard sizes are 1 inch in diameter, 12 or 18 inches in length, and come in 30- and 40-watt capacities.

Decorative Bulbs

Some light bulbs are decorative and distinctive in themselves. This is true of the *F-bulbs* (*flame-shaped*) and the *G-bulbs* (*globe-shaped*). Others, like the smaller sizes of reflector bulbs, may be used to add color effects to your decor or to provide accent lighting on unusual or artistic decorative features.

Flame-shaped bulbs might be called "electrified candles." They are designed for wall sconces, candelabras, and chandeliers to supply a warm glow of candlelight throughout a room. Clean glass F-bulbs particularly simulate candle flames. And if you want subtle variety, you can find it among the many modified shapes and colors of F-bulbs—some with bent tips to carry out the illusion of a flaming candle and some with straight-sided flame shapes, which could be a concession to modernists

Designer: Walter Dunivant Photography: Harold Davis

This Charmglow pest control unit, above left, has 30 watts of insect-attracting black light output with a 5000-volt grid charge. The all-plastic top and enclosure measure 12" x 12" x 18". This model is for use in larger backyard areas. It comes in natural color tones to blend with backyard settings.

The flame-shaped bulbs in the photo above right shed a warm glow of candlelight to enhance the mood of romantic dining. This chandelier is an example of a fixture that is not readily accessible and that would benefit from long-lasting flame-shaped bulbs.

still in love with candlelight. The variety of bulb styles, all conforming to the basic flame shape, along with the range of sizes, will satisfy many moods and decorative desires. The choice is even widened with the many subtle glass colors available in these lamps, as well as the capacity sizes which generally range from 15 to 16 watts.

In considering the use of flame-shaped bulbs, special attention should be given to the type and size of the base with which they are fitted. Many types are available in the medium screw base that is common to most general service lamps. Some, however, are fitted with candelabra bases that call for special sockets in the fixtures.

Since the use of flame-shaped lamps can be considered mood lighting, it should be recognized that their light output can be adjusted easily by the inclusion of a dimmer in the control circuit.

G-Bulbs (*globe-shaped*) offer even more flexibility in lighting effects than do the F-bulbs. Their use is not restricted solely to filling lighting fixture sockets. They can be installed in their bare state on the surfaces of walls and ceilings to provide general illumination. The sockets or fittings are usually buried.

Globe bulbs bring a modern feeling to any interior. They definitely add a contemporary look. Globe sizes range from 2 1/6 inches to 6 inches in diameter. Wattages run from 15 to 150 watts in clear or white bulbs and from 25 to 100 watts in colored glass, gold, or silver mirrored surfaces.

Special Incandescent Lamps

The lineup of light bulbs would not be complete without a mention of some one-purpose lamps. In this category are: *bug lamps*, *heat lamps*, *sun lamps*, *plant lamps*, and *appliance* and *indicator lamps*.

Bug lamps, coated with yellow enamel, emit yellow and red light rays that repel insects. They are used on patios, decks, terraces, and balconies where night-flying insects are prevalent. They are available in 40-, 60-, and 100-watt sizes.

Heat lamps are reflector lamps with special red bowls that assure maximum emission of infrared rays. Popular applications are on bathroom ceilings for space heating or on covered outdoor areas to provide comfortable warmth. Heat lamps have a therapeutic value in treating

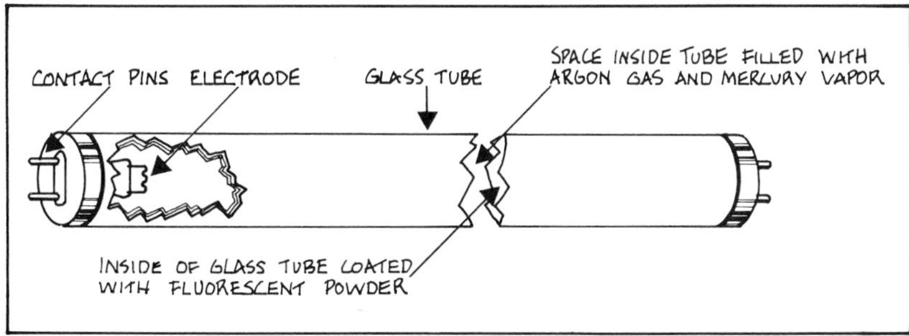

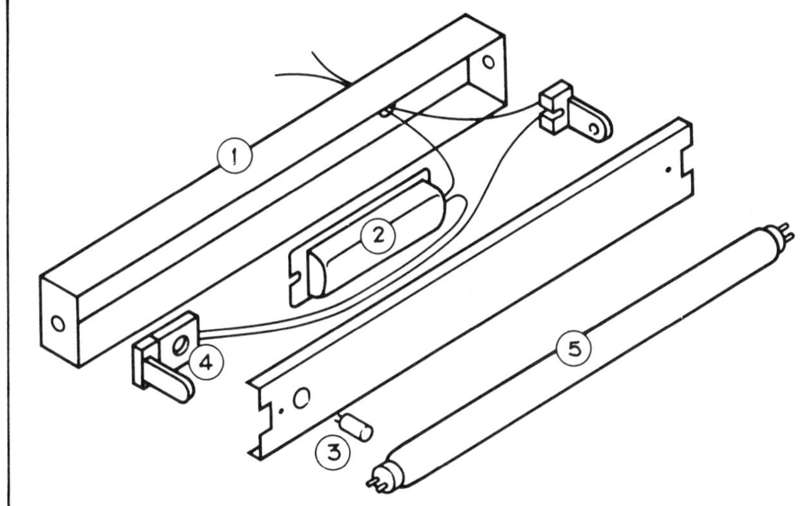

Here are the basic elements of a conventional fluorescent fixture:

1. **METAL CHANNEL — the box used to hold it all together.**
2. **BALLAST — may be mounted some distance away.**
3. **STARTER — required with all conventional ballasts, lamps.**
4. **LAMPHOLDERS — must be properly spaced for the length of fluorescent tube used.**
5. **FLUORESCENT LAMP — select for proper color and wattage.**

Fluorescent lighting components required for custom lighting applications are shown here. There is a wide variety of prewired metal fixtures for fluorescent lighting, and it's best to make use of these assemblies whenever possible. But there are some applications where space simply won't permit the use of these assemblies, and the only alternative is to make your own.

The fluorescent bulb, top, shows the elements that include a long narrow glass cylinder coated on the interior with any of several types of phosphor. A phosphor is a special chemical compound that emits light when activated by energy. Air in the tube is replaced with mercury vapor and argon, an inert gas.

muscular soreness. The skin is not only warmed, but the infrared rays penetrate the surface to the muscles below. Heat lamps are useful in the home workshop for chores such as setting glue or cemented joints or speeding up removal of floor tile or old furniture finishes. For home use, heat lamps are available in the 250-watt size with 5-inch bowls.

Reflector sun lamps outwardly resemble a standard 5-inch reflector lamp. Within the outside bulb is a special glass bulb containing a mercury arc that provides the ultraviolet suntan rays. This *RS* bulb, with its medium screw base, fits into any ordinary household socket and uses 275 watts. Its normal life is 1,000 15-minute application periods.

Appliance and indicator bulbs are designed to fit into the restricted spaces of home appliances. They are used in such cold spaces as refrigerators and freezers or for the high temperature conditions in ovens, rotisseries, etc. For home use, appliance bulbs come in the 15-, 25-, and 40-watt sizes.

Indicator lamps serve many signaling and indicating functions that add convenience and safety to home appliances and electrical equipment. In replacing burnt-out indicator lamps, the type of socket, lamp base, bulb size, and wattage should be noted for accurate reordering. The safest plan is to take the old bulb as a sample when you shop for a replacement.

Fluorescent Tubes

When *Daylight fluorescent tubes* were introduced in the 1930s, lighting engineers and lamp designers took great pride in the fact that they had made "daylight" available any hour of the day or night. Daylight fluorescent light was accepted quite readily for use in industrial plants and offices, and later retail stores experimented with its use.

The lamp industry was particularly elated that they had made a major breakthrough in lighting efficiency. The 40-watt daylight fluorescent tube would produce a 4-foot sheet of light with an emission of about 2,500 lumens and an estimated life of 3,000 hours. In contrast, the 40-watt incandescent bulb of that period produced a spot of light amounting to about 350 lumens with a life of approximately 1,200 hours.

Even today, it must be recognized

A

Watts	Tube Diameter	Tube Length	Lumens Deluxe Colors*	Lumens Standard Colors*	Average Life-Hours
15	1″	18″	610	870	7,500
15	1½″	18″	540	800	9,000
20	1½″	24″	850	1300	9,000
30	1″	36″	1540	2300	18,000
40	1½″	48″	2150	3150	20,000

B

Watts	Tube Diameter	Tube Length	Lumens Range	Average Life-Hours
40	1½″	22¼″	1980-2900	12,000

C

Watts	Tube Diameter	Circle Diameter	Lumens Range	Average Life-Hours
20	2″	6½″	650-825	12,000
22	2¼″	8¼″	800-1000	12,000
32	2¼″	12″	1300-1900	12,000
40	2¼″	16″	1900-2600	12,000

D

	Watts	Lumen Output	Average Life-Hours
Fluorescent	44	1750	7,500
Incandescent	100	1750	750

that there is an inherent difference in efficiency and life between 40-watt incandescent and 40-watt daylight fluorescent lamps. Today's comparison works out this way:

Type	Watts	Lumens	Life-Hours
Fluorescent	40	3150	20,000
Incandescent	40	480	1,500

A *fluorescent tube* is radically different in shape and construction from an incandescent bulb. A sealed glass tube coated on the inside with a combination of phosphorescent powders, it contains a small amount of inert gas and mercury vapor. When the lamp is activated, the mercury vapor becomes an arc producing ultraviolet rays. These rays cause the phosphorescent coating on the inside to glow and emit rays of a determined color value.

One important characteristic of the light rays given off by a fluorescent tube is that they are a combination of the phosphorescent color glow and the mercury arc wave lengths that come through the porous phosphor coating. The arc wave lengths are predominantly yellow-green and violet and account for about 10 percent of the light output. The light emission from standard white fluorescent tubes contains an appreciable amount of mercury arc colors. Deluxe white lamps have a coating of phosphors that offset, to a great degree, the arc emissions.

Fluorescent tubes differ, too, from incandescent bulbs in their need for special types of fixtures. Only one type, described later, can be screwed into a common light socket. The rest of the fluorescent lamps have special bases and also an electric circuit that is controlled by one or more ballasts (transformers) built into the fixtures holding the tubes.

General service fluorescent tubes commonly used in homes are the straight *white* lamps ranging in length from 18 to 48 inches. These are known as *preheat fluorescent lamps* for use in fixtures with starters or fixtures containing starterless quick starting circuits. Operating characteristics for this type of fluorescent tube are shown in chart A.

*Lumen output values are for *white* lamps. Deluxe lamps provide good color quality in both *warm* and *cool* tones for more accurate color renditions.

E

Watts	Tube Diameter	Tube Length	Average Life
20	1½"	24"	5000 applications
40	1½"	48"	15 minutes per start

F

Watts	Tube Diameter	Tube Length	Average Life-Hours
20	1½"	24"	9,000
40	1½"	48"	20,000

G

Watts	Tube Diameter	Tube Length	Average Life-Hours
4	⅝"	6"	6,000
6	⅝"	9"	7,500
8	⅝"	12"	7,500
15	1"	18"	7,500
20	1½"	24"	9,000
30	1"	36"	7,500
40	1½"	48"	20,000

H

Watts	Tube Diameter	Tube Length	Average Life-Hours	Lumen Output
15	1"	18"	7,500	410
20	1½"	24"	9,000	600
40	1½"	48"	20,000	1,600

New shapes in fluorescent tubes were developed to supplement the straight line tubes. They have allowed fixture designers to depart from the common lines of light and rectangular lighting fixtures. U-shaped lamps, formed by bending a 4-foot standard tube, come with two leg spacings: 3 5/8 inches and 6 inches. The reason for these leg spacings is that either two or three of these bent lamps can be used in a 2-foot-square ceiling fixture.

Operating characteristics of these tubes are shown in chart B.

Circular fluorescent lamps are found in portable and ceiling fixtures today in four ring sizes. Operating characteristics of these *Circle Lights* are shown in chart C.

A recent innovation by *General Electric Co.* is a circular fluorescent lamp that can be screwed into an ordinary socket. It is billed as the lamp that "could render obsolete the ordinary incandescent light bulb in a multitude of table lamps and ceiling fixtures." Its color emission is similar to that of an incandescent household bulb. Chart D shows how the 44-watt *Circlite* gives as much light as a 100-watt incandescent bulb and lasts 10 times longer.

Specialty Fluorescent Lamps

Most of the specialty fluorescent lamps take advantage of the mercury arc, which is the activating force in the tube. The arc not only causes the phosphor coating to glow, but it produces ultraviolet radiation, which can be very useful.

Fluorescent sunlamps outwardly look like standard fluorescent lamps with a bluish-white tube. Operating characteristics are shown in chart E.

Fluorescent bug lamps cast a yellow glow that is repellant to night-flying insects. They come in two sizes and can be hung over a patio, deck, or terrace. Operating characteristics are shown in chart F.

Fluorescent germicidal lamps generate bactericidal or germicidal ultraviolet radiation. They have no phosphor coating and are made with a special glass that transmits the germicidal rays emitted by the mercury arc within the tube. One common home application of germicidal lamps is to place them at the intake location in an air conditioning flue to destroy airborne bacteria. Also known as *black lights*, the output of these lamps will cause phosphor pigment in a mural or other surface to glow for a decorative effect.

Guide for use of general household bulbs

These guides will give you the right light with the least energy consumption.

1. *25 watt.* Suspended pendants of 5- or 6-inch diameter. Lantern with frosted glass globe or chimney. Mantle brackets. TV lamp.
2. *40 watt.* Bedroom or dining room fixtures with four or five sockets. Hall fixtures with three sockets. Multi-socket bath mirror brackets. Portable lamps with three or more sockets.
3. *60 watt.* Multiglobe ceiling fixture. Three-socket kitchen "drum type" ceiling fixture. Single-socket bath mirror brackets. Vestibule ceiling fixture or bracket.
4. *75 watt.* Post or patio light. Two in fixture over sink, or behind a cornice board. Three-socket portable lamp.
5. *100 watt.* Dressing table or dresser lamps. Wall lamps over study desk. Hanging fixture in kitchen or dinette. Two-socket portable lamp.
6. *150 watt.* Large luminous hanging "bubble." Reading lamp, one-way socket, recessed fixtures. Kitchen ceiling globe. Garage or storage area.
7. *200 watt.* Reading lamp with 8-inch diffusing bowl. Kitchen globe—14 to 16 inches in diameter. Garage or storage area. Better Light Better Sight (BLBS) study lamp.

Illustration source: General Electric

Operating characteristics are shown in chart G on page 33.

Fluorescent plant lamps with a special phosphor blend supply house plants with radiant energy most conducive to plant growth and early blooming. Operating characteristics are shown in chart H on page 33.

The Color Question

For general lighting use there is no color emission problem in selecting incandescent bulbs. They all give off a strong candlelight. Colored incandescent bulbs are generally used for accent lighting, not for general household illumination.

When the original *daylight fluorescent tubes* were first available, women's complaints of sallow complexions and an unhealthy look were justified. Lamp design engineers eliminated such complaints with the introduction of warm-tone fluorescent lamps with more natural and accurate color rendition.

Today, the question of what fluorescent *white light* to select can be a rather confusing proposition. One major lamp manufacturer lists 15 fluorescent *white lamps* as readily available. Some of these have been developed for special applications in store displays and in color-sensitive industrial operations. From a practical standpoint, a homemaker has the following fluorescent white lamps to choose from: *Daylight, Cool White, Deluxe Cool White, Warm White, Deluxe Warm White,* and *Soft White.*

Daylight fluorescent lamps for general lighting in a home are being used mostly in those climates with excessively high temperatures. The blue-white glow psychologically creates a cool atmosphere. This color is *not* recommended for use with supplementary incandescent lighting.

Cool white fluorescent lamps, as the name indicates, provide cool illumination without the bluish tinge that comes from daylight tubes. Cool white is still lacking in the degree of true color rendition desired by discriminating homemakers.

Deluxe cool white has the highest degree of color rendition of the cool lamps. For those desiring a cool atmosphere in their home during the summer months, it offers a practical blend with incandescent lighting.

Warm white fluorescent lamps were the first breakaway from daylight tubes. They did give off a warmer tone of light that was more compatible with incandescent light-

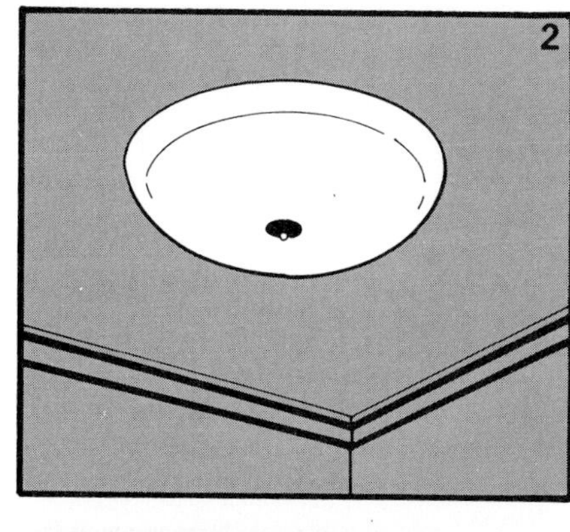

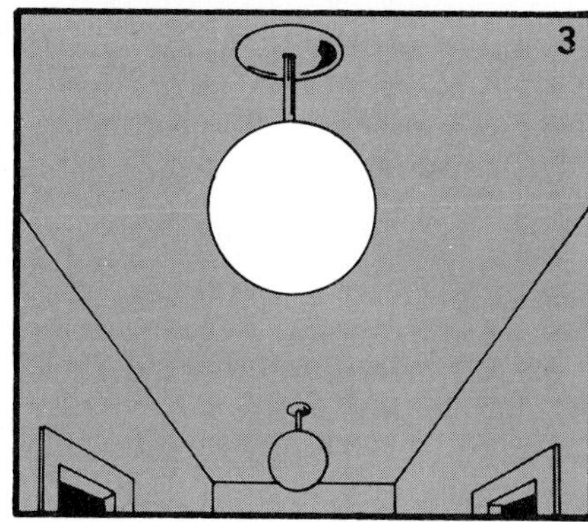

ing. Their color rendition was the most accurate of fluorescent lamps at the time.

Deluxe warm white fluorescent lamps were the next step by lamp manufacturers in improving fluorescent color rendition. These seemed to be the ultimate in color correction for home use. However, lamp designers were not satisfied and continued their research.

Soft white fluorescent lamps are being recommended by manufacturers as the ideal companion in home lighting with *soft white incandescent* bulbs. One company lists these lamps as *Soft White Home Fluorescent*. The advantages are that it blends well with incandescent lighting, it flatters complexions, it creates a cozy atmosphere, and it highlights the warm colors used in many homes.

From these descriptions of the color output of fluorescent lamps, it would seem that the deluxe cool lamps and the soft white lamps would satisfy the needs of most homemakers for general fluorescent illumination. If the soft white color is not available in some types and sizes needed for your special application, the deluxe warm white lamps may prove to be an acceptable substitute.

Designer: Barbara Lerner
Photography: Harold Davis

The lighting in this kitchen shows the results of careful analysis. The combination of natural light from the skylight and artificial light from the built-in recessed fixtures provides good general illumination. Individual focal points are emphasized by adequate task lighting.

4 Your Lighting Plan

You may feel somewhat uncertain about the proper steps needed to design a lighting system for your new home or incorporate lighting improvements in a remodeling project. Such apprehension is understandable because you will be dealing with the rather complex relationships of light and shadow, colors, and textures.

This complexity need not be overwhelming even to a novice homemaker. There is a logical step-by-step method of relating your lighting needs to the way you and your family live and to the decorating scheme you are most comfortable with and are able to afford.

Your lighting plan starts with some very basic thinking. It is most important that you determine how you and your family will use your home and each room within it. This calls for a careful analysis of your lifestyle. Each individual and every family has interests and preferences which should be considered. A thorough investigation of the various activities that take place in your home, by your family as a whole and by each family member, will uncover much about your lighting needs.

Conduct your room-by-room analysis with pencil and note pad in hand. For a new home, mentally walk through the plans picturing each room and how it will be used. A remodeling project is usually easier to examine, since you can physically check the intensity and direction of light streaming through the window or locate existing electrical outlets while determining who will use the room and what activities will take place in it.

Rather than trying to develop a master checklist for this project, the following examples will provide you with the kind of questions to ask yourself and what to look for on your room-by-room analysis.

Is a dining room or living room part of your everyday family activity or are they used only for formal occasions and entertaining? When you entertain, is it for small, intimate groups or full-blown family get-togethers? Do you prefer sit-down dinners with your best china and candlelight or do you usually have buffet meals in a more relaxed setting?

Is the master bedroom used for sleeping only, or is it also used as a dressing area, letter-writing and reading area? At bedtime, do you like to read yourself to sleep but your spouse likes the room dimly lit so he can drop off to sleep immediately? Will your lighting arrangement satisfy both of you?

Is the bathroom purely functional or does it also serve as a grooming and makeup area? Is the mirror lighting compatible with masculine shaving and feminine makeup requirements?

What is the age category of individuals using a particular space? Young children need more general lighting in play areas and less lamps to knock over. Teenagers require well-lighted study areas while elderly individuals prefer a reading lamp beside a comfortable chair and may need better intensity and quality of lighting to bolster their failing eyesight.

As you conduct your survey, record the information necessary to plan a satisfying lighting system. You will know where functional lighting is required for difficult seeing tasks.

Photography: Harold Davis Designer: Cannell and Chaffin

Photography: Westinghouse Electric

A lighting plan involves taking a careful survey of your needs room by room. For a living room like the one above left, you would need to ask yourself these questions: Is this room part of my everyday family activity? Is it used only for formal or informal occasions? When I entertain, is it for small or large groups?

The dining room above right demonstrates the kind of formal lighting that suits sit-down dinners with your best china and candlelight. The decorative accents of the china collection are highlighted by the cabinet display lighting.

You will be reminded that a bridge game, poker session, pool or ping-pong game will be more enjoyable if properly lighted. Decorative accents such as pictures, statuary, collections, and bookshelves should call attention to themselves subtly when special illumination is provided. All such localized lighting should be supplemented with unobtrusive general illumination to provide a tasteful balance of brightness values.

Livable Lighting

As you record lighting needs and preferences, make notes covering any flexibility in the use of various rooms and open spaces. Is that extra bedroom always used as a guest room? Is it a part-time guest room that is also used as a sewing room or playroom? Such diversity of use points up the fact that the lighting requirements in any particular room may change radically overnight.

Part of your room-by-room analysis should be a consideration of furnishing and color schemes. Will these remain the same or do you plan a new look for some rooms?

Not to be overlooked in your lifestyle analysis are cost and budget estimates. Start your light planning with a general dollar figure in mind and determine what you can afford to spend to carry out your plans.

A complete analysis, as suggested, should give you a thorough understanding of your family's preferences and requirements. In fact, you may find some surprises as you add up the needs and desires of the various family members. It is helpful to define your desired lifestyle in simple terms. Is it a quiet, conservative way of life keyed to the home interests of mature, adult individuals? Or must the needs and activities of several generations under the same roof be catered to in an expensive way? When these questions are answered, you will be ready to proceed with the development of an appropriate lighting plan.

A well-thought-out lighting plan can enhance your family home in a number of ways. Starting at your entrance, it can offer your guests a cordial welcome. It can provide a restful, relaxing atmosphere for everyday living. It can create a festive mood for special occasions. The right plan can subtly suggest the individuality of distinctive decor. All of this can be provided while safeguarding precious eyesight with adequate and

Footcandle Conversion Chart

35mm camera exposure meter set at ASA 100. Shutter speed set at 1/30th of a second.

Position a large white card at a 45-degree angle to the light source. Card should be at table, counter, or work bench height—approximately 28-30 inches from the floor.

Fill the camera view finder with the white card image taking care not to cast a shadow on card. Use the table below to translate meter reading into approximate footcandle light level. Do *not* aim meter directly at light source.

Meter Reading	Footcandles
f 1.4	5
f 1.8	7.5
f 2	10
f 3.5	15
f 4	20
f 4.5	30
f 5.6	40
f 6.3	60
f 8	80
f 9	120
f 11	160
f 14	240
f 16	320
f 18	480
f 22	640

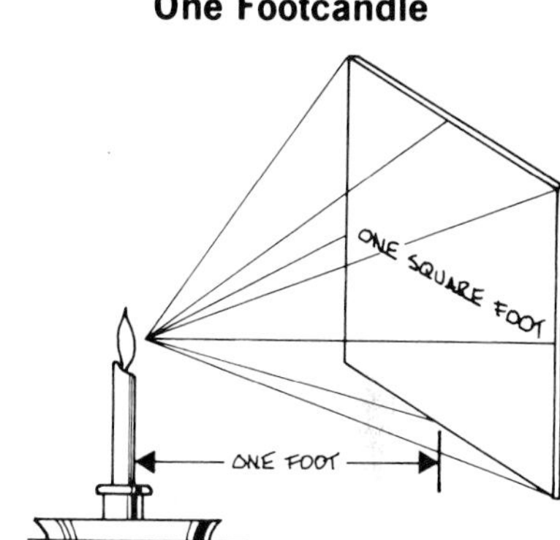

appropriate lighting throughout your home for critical seeing tasks.

Adequate Lighting

The term *lumens* has been used in previous chapters to show the output of light sources. One lumen is defined as the amount of light reaching a surface, one square foot in size, at a distance of one foot from the flame of a "standard candle." Such a standard candle has definite specifications for the composition of the wax and the rate at which it burns. It is known as a *Candela* from the Latin word meaning candle.

Some idea of the amount of illumination provided by an artificial light source can be gained from the fact that a 75-watt light bulb provides 30 footcandles of light on a surface 3 feet from the source. It may be helpful to know that on a clear summer day direct sunlight may deliver more than 10,000 footcandles on a beach or open field, 200 footcandles inside a house a few feet from a window, and only 10 footcandles in the center of a house away from all windows.

The amount of light reaching a surface can be measured directly with a hand-held instrument known as a *footcandle meter*. It is about the size of a camera exposure meter. The price of such a meter ranges from $35 to $55. You can get information on buying a *footcandle meter* through the district office of one of the major lamp manufacturers. You may be able to borrow a meter from the Customer Service Department of your local electric utility company or from someone you know in the business.

If you are unable to buy or borrow a professional *footcandle meter*, there is a convenient substitute that will give you a reasonably accurate illumination reading on critical work surfaces in your home. The table conversion, shown above, was developed by a professional photographer using a 35mm standard camera exposure meter.

By using a *footcandle meter* or an exposure meter, you can be assured that the lighting devices and fixtures you select will do two things: They will accommodate bulbs or tubes large enough to provide the desired light intensities and will also project those intensities onto the working or other surfaces.

Recommended Illumination Levels

The illumination levels listed on

A convenient substitute for a professional footcandle meter is shown above left, using a standard 35mm camera exposure meter to measure the amount of light reaching a surface area.

The illustration above right will help you visualize one footcandle of light (candela)—the amount of light thrown on one square foot of surface that is one foot away.

Modern lighting in the kitchen above is an integral part of the overall sleek, functional, and tasteful design. The white marble work island and Allmilmo cabinets brighten the effect, but are saved from appearing cold by a successful lighting plan.

this page for various tasks are those recommended by *The Illuminating Engineering Society* as being "the minimum at any time" levels. As any lamp burns, there is a slight decrease in light output as it ages. Since your selection of light sources and fixtures will be dealing with the *initial* output, the IES levels have been increased about 20 percent to assure that both initial levels and minimum levels over the life of the lamp will be attained. For instance, the IES minimum standard of 50 footcandles for kitchen work counters has been increased to 60 footcandles for an initial lighting level.

Specific Visual Task	Initial Foot-candles
Table games	40
Kitchen sink, food preparation areas	150
Kitchen work surface, range	60
Laundry, ironing board	60
Reading, Writing, Studying	
Books, magazines, newspapers	40
Handwriting, reproductions (poor copies)	85
Study desks	85
Reading Music Scores	
Simple scores	35
Advanced scores	85
Sewing	
Occasional periods, coarse thread, large stitches	40
Occasional periods, light fabrics	60
Prolonged periods, light to medium fabrics	120
Dark fabrics, fine detail, low contrast	240
Grooming	
Makeup, shaving, on face at mirror location	60
Work Shop	
Bench work	85
For General Lighting	
Entrances, hallways, stairways, stair landings, living room, dining room, bedroom, family room	12
Sun room, library, game room, recreation room	12
Kitchen, laundry, bathroom, workshop	60

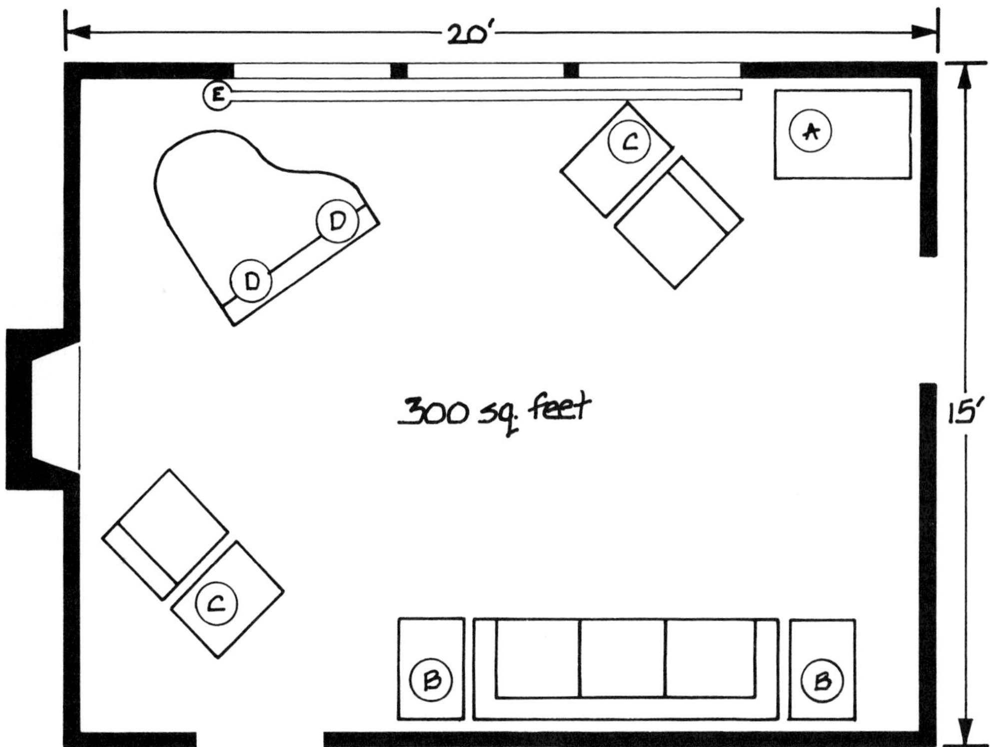

This plan shows the required lumens in a living room 15' x 20'. To determine the lumens, multiply the area (300 sq. ft.) by the recommended lumens per square feet for a living room (80). This figure is 24,000 total lumens.

The footcandle values given for specific visual tasks are those for a kitchen counter, a desk top, a book page, a face looking into a mirror—all the surfaces that require high intensity illumination. If this were the only lighting provided in a room, it would produce eye strain from glare spots in dim surroundings. To avoid this, general lighting is recommended to supplement the *working lights*. By filling a room with plenty of general lighting, shadows on various work surfaces are ultimately eliminated or comfortably softened.

Home lighting experts have devised a simple method of achieving an adequate and comfortable blend of local and general lighting sources. The *lumens required per square foot* for various rooms and areas in a home are provided in the chart below:

Living Room	80
Dining Room	45
Kitchen	80
Bathroom	65
Bedroom	70
Hallway	45
Laundry	70
Work Bench Area	70

These are the recommended lumens when a room is lighted by a combination of portable lamps, surface-mounted fixtures, and structural lighting techniques. Light sources recessed in cornices, or valances, the top of a high bookcase are termed structural lighting.
If a high percentage of the total illumination comes from recessed light sources, experts recommend the lumen requirements be doubled.

Illustrated above is an example of the *required lumens* method applied to a typical suburban living room that is 15 by 20 feet in size. The room is furnished to satisfy a mother who carries on a large correspondence with friends across the country, a father who likes informal gatherings of close friends and neighbors, and a daughter who is studying music at a local college. This is the lifestyle of this particular family as applied to the living room above.

To determine the total lumens needed in this room, multiply the area (300 square feet) by the recommended lumens per square foot for a living room (80). This figure is 24,000 total lumens. Illumination breakdown for each location in the room follows:

Electrical Symbols for Home Lighting Plans

General Outlets

- ○ Ceiling surface fixture outlet
- ◎ Ceiling recessed fixture outlet
- Continuous wireway for fluorescent lighting on ceiling, in coves, cornices, etc. (Extend rectangle to show length of installation.)

Convenience Outlets

- Duplex convenience outlet
- GR Duplex convenience outlet for grounding-type plug
- WP Weatherproof convenience outlet
- S Combination switch and convenience outlet
- ⊙ Floor outlet

Switch Outlets

- S Single-pole switch
- S_3 Three-way switch
- S_4 Four-way switch
- S_D Automatic door switch
- S_{WP} Weatherproof switch

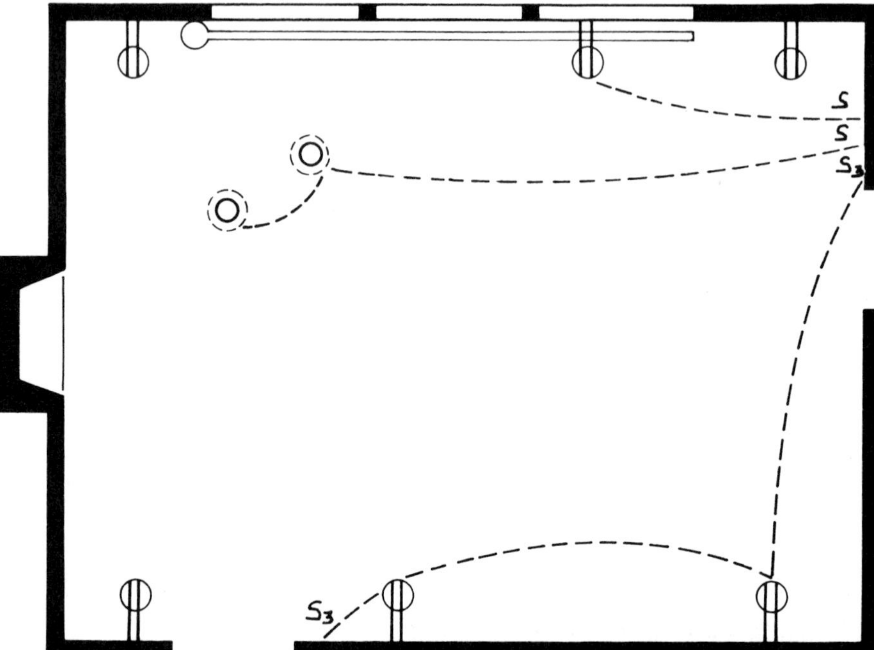

The wiring plan for the living room above is keyed to the lighting plan shown on the previous page. It provides a great deal of flexibility in using the various pieces of lighting equipment. On and off switching for the lighting circuits is supplemented by the 3-way bulbs in the lamps.

	Lumens
A. One 200-watt inside frosted bulb at 3,940 lumens in a study lamp	3,940
B. Two (50-200-250-watt) Soft White 3-way bulbs at 4,110 lumens each in two senior table lamps	8,220
C. Two (50-100-150-watt) Soft White 3-way bulbs at 2,190 lumens in two chairside table lamps	4,380
D. Two 75-watt reflector spotlights ceiling recessed at 860 lumens each over the piano keyboard ...	1,720
E. Three 40-watt Deluxe Warm White fluorescent tubes at 2,080 lumens each in a drapery cornice	6,240
Total Lumens Provided	**24,500**

Shown above, the wiring plan for this living room is keyed to the lighting plan. It provides a great flexibility in using the various pieces of lighting equipment. On and off switching for the lighting circuits is supplemented by the 3-way bulbs in the lamps with low, medium, and high controls. The only set of lights in the room that might have dimmer controls would be the fluorescent cornice tubes for mood lighting.

This typical lighting plan for an average living room and its related wiring plan covers the basic technical steps to achieve an adequate and flexible lighting system for any room. The specifications for portable lamps, fixtures, and lighting equipment, as yet, have not considered the contribution that they can make to the decorating scheme in a room.

At this point in the planning process, it is advisable to firm up your specifications for the general types of portable lamps already selected. Your final choice should definitely include:

—The size and shape of the lamp base and shade so it is compatible with the room's furnishings.

—The manner in which the lamp's light source is shielded to prevent glare in anyone's eyes while sitting or standing near the lamp.

—The assurance that the lamp is equipped with the size and type of socket needed for the specific light source such as a 3-way bulb.

Energy Conservation Planning

Your lighting plan and the wiring system for any room can contribute to real energy savings. Three-way

Light Planning and Conservation Tips

Regardless of whether you're doing it yourself or hiring professionals, remodeling or building a new home, you'll find it pays to keep the following planning and conservation tips in mind:

1. Avoid using a higher wattage bulb than recommended. Look for information on the inside of the fixture.
2. Get the most light for your dollar. Buy the wattage bulb you need, but compare the lumen ratings and select the bulb that produces the most lumens in that wattage.
3. Use fluorescent tubes for an efficient lighting system. Select the longest tube that will fit the space.
4. Use local lighting in combination with general lighting to prevent working in your own shadow.
5. Use white, coated bulbs in ceiling fixtures to provide well-diffused light.
6. For visual comfort, always select fixtures that shield the bulb from view.
7. Make sure there is a balance of general and local lighting.
8. In planning, be sure that there are not excessive differences in the illumination between adjoining rooms.
9. Use dimmer controls to create pleasing effects and save electricity at the same time.
10. For maximum efficiency, replace bulbs before they burn out. Blackened bulbs produce less light than new ones, but use the same amount of electricity.
11. Plan your decorating scheme to take advantage of light-reflecting surfaces. Dark colors absorb light while white or pastel colors reflect light.
12. Use deluxe fluorescent tubes to enhance your color schemes—deluxe cool white with greens and blues, deluxe warm white with reds, oranges.
13. Provide switch controls at all entry and exit points in the room.
14. Turn lights off if the room is unoccupied.
15. For best efficiency, keep light bulbs and fixtures free of dust and dirt.

bulbs in the four table lamps will generally be switched to low or medium intensities. Only when you want a "blaze of lights" in the room for some special occasion will these lamps be on the high setting. Functional lighting for the writing desk and the piano music rack will seldom be on at the same time, and rarely when all the rest of the lighting is being used. Thus, the flexibility of use built into lighting and wiring plans assures conservative use of the facilities. At the same time the family has the benefit of adequate and comfortable lighting.

Throughout any home there are numerous ways to minimize the use of electricity for lighting. The most obvious way, often neglected, is to turn off the lighting when it is no longer needed. Fluorescent tubes, with their more efficient light output, can in some instances be acceptable substitutes for incandescent bulbs. The use of 3-way bulbs is an excellent means of using only the amount of light that circumstances call for. Dimmer controls inserted in lighting circuits function in the same way. Lamp manufacturers are now producing long-life and energy-saving bulbs and tubes.

Photography: Harold Davis
Designer: John Frendling, ASID

The decorative scheme of this living room called for bold salmon-colored walls with a striking contrast of white accents. Carefully selected lamps, fixtures, and bulbs serve to enhance the decor, not detract from it. A sense of warmth is achieved by combining the salmon color with soft white lighting.

5 Light for Decorating

The use of light to enhance your home decor and reflect your personality is the fun aspect of lighting. It can be a rather intriguing and satisfying experience if you are willing to give free rein to your artistic and creative desires. It offers you the opportunity to develop a distinctive pattern of lighting which demonstrates your family lifestyle. It can be a means of enhancing or changing moods as you wish.

To achieve all these elements involves careful attention to a number of basic factors. The interplay of light and color is so sensitive that the slightest change in the color tone of the lighting source makes a marked change in the apparent color of room surfaces. Also, the surface characteristics of the materials and fabrics, rough or smooth, shiny or dull, can appear to change if the predominant light beam is changed. The brightness of any object or surface can be comfortable or uncomfortable to a viewer depending on its contrast with its surroundings. It seems then that the various combinations of these factors can result in different outward appearances of objects and surfaces.

A word of caution seems appropriate at this point. In any remodeling of a lighting system and redoing of a decorating scheme, or in planning for a new home, many critical decisions must be made. Individual decisions affect the plan as a whole and can help or hurt the project. If the color of a painted wall is found to be wrong when the lights are turned on, the cost of paint materials and labor to rectify the error will be substantial.

Color Is How You Light It

When the wall of a room is painted blue, you might think it would always look the same shade of blue. But view it under three different "white" lights and it seems as though it had been painted three different shades of blue. Daylight, incandescent light, and fluorescent light, in turn, apparently change the basic color of the wall surface.

Or, view two pieces of fabric dyed the same color, one that has a velvet texture, the other a smooth satin finish, and when placed side by side under the same color of light, they seem to be of different colors.

These two examples seem to indicate that the subject of light and color is a rather confusing proposition. To avoid this confusion you must keep in mind one basic principle—the color of any object or surface is the color of light bouncing back or being transmitted through it. If you always remember this basic truth, you will find that you have the ability to manipulate colors by controlling the characteristics of light sources. With this understanding of the interplay of light and color, you have acquired a valuable tool.

Since part of the light striking a surface or passing through it is absorbed, the brightness of the surface is determined by the light that reaches the eye by reflection or transmission. The partial absorption of the light wavelengths in some cases will actually change the color impression reaching the eye, as well as reducing the brightness of the lighted surface.

Three white-light sources have been recommended previously as

Color Rendition

	Incandescent Soft White	**Fluor. Deluxe Warm White**	**Fluor. Deluxe Cool White**
Appearance effect on neutral surfaces	Yellowish white	Yellowish white	White
Effect on "atmosphere"	Warm	Warm	Moderately cool
Colors strengthened	Red, Orange Yellow	Red, Orange Yellow, Green	All nearly equal
Colors grayed	Blue	Blue	None appreciably
Effects on complexions	Ruddiest	Ruddy	Most natural
Remarks	Good color rendition	Good color rendition; simulates incandescent light	Best color rendition; simulates natural daylight

those that will satisfy the usual illumination needs throughout most homes. They are: *Incandescent Soft White* and *Fluorescent Deluxe Warm White* and *Deluxe Cool White*. These are accepted as having *good* color rendition qualities. The term *good rendition* is generally interpreted to mean the *familiar* appearance of household objects. And because we are most familiar with the appearance of objects under daylight or incandescent light, we accept both types of light sources as giving good color rendition and producing a *normal* appearance. This familiarity of a *cool* appearance under daylight and of a *warm* appearance under incandescent light as both being *normal* is certainly contradictory. It has been rationalized for years by stating that both appearances are familiar ones. Some lighting experts believe that if fluorescent lighting had come into wide use before incandescent, colors would seem most familiar to people under the tubes.

Any questions you have had about normal color appearance should be answered now, after reading the color rendition analysis given above.

In any room of your house, color rendition from light sources is subject to more modification than indicated in the simple analysis just presented. The light emitted from bulbs and tubes in most instances does not reach an object or surface directly. Its color qualities are modified to some extent by the light waves being reflected from colored surfaces or being transmitted through the shades on fixtures and portable lamps. If natural daylight is streaming in the window and artificial light is used also, the apparent colors of the surroundings may be modified further. Fortunately, such color modifications are usually relatively slight and would be detected only by a trained eye.

If you are working out a decorative scheme involving bold, striking colors with much contrast, even slight modifications of color appearances might reduce its effectiveness. In such a case, the advice of a lighting expert could be helpful.

At this point you may ask, "How can I be sure the colors selected for my decorating scheme will look right under my home lighting?" The answer to that is, "See for yourself."

"Light booths," as they are known in the lighting field, are used for color-matching or the selection of

Homemade Color Comparison Box

Behind top valance:

Left Box	—Fluorescent 14-watt, T-12, 15-inch Deluxe Cool White Tube. Wiring strip with sockets, starter, ballast, line switch
Center box	—Incandescent 40-watt Soft-White Bulb with socket and line switch
Right Box	—Fluorescent 14-watt, T-12, 15-inch Deluxe Warm White Tube. Wiring strip with sockets, starter, ballast, line switch

Six-foot electrical cord with standard plug. Interior surfaces of boxes painted a good quality flat white.

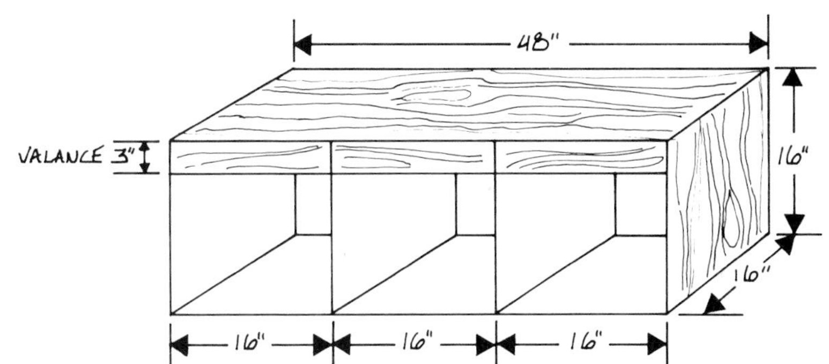

colors under different tones of light. They are simple box-like compartments next to each other, lighted by the different light source colors under consideration (see the photo in chapter 7 on page 79).

Any adept do-it-yourselfer can put together a composite set of three comparison light boxes at reasonable cost. A convenient size for home use would have overall dimensions of 48 inches wide, 16 inches high, and 16 inches deep, all painted with flat white interior surfaces and equipped with the following light sources:

- ☐ **Left box** — Fluorescent 14-watt T-12 Deluxe cool White Tube
- ☐ **Center box** — Incandescent 40-watt Soft White Bulb
- ☐ **Right box** — Fluorescent 14-watt T-12 Deluxe Warm White Tube

With such a set of comparison boxes, you will be able to make your own evaluations of the relative color renditions of various decorating materials and colors. Your decorator, flooring, or fabric shop can furnish sample swatches for your inspection. Your painter or paint supplier can give you color cards or make up special color mixtures for your use. To make your own comparison light box, see the sketch above.

Living Room Lighting

General

1. Establish an adequate general illumination level to reduce accent light brightness contrast.
2. Illuminate an entire wall with overhead track fixtures or with wall washers to provide background for room furnishings.
3. Feature window areas with valance or cornice lighting.
4. Indirect cove lighting will supply soft, uniform illumination.
5. Use dimmers and 3-way bulbs to program lighting moods.

Accent

1. Play up architectural features, pitched ceilings, alcoves, fireplace, and mantel.
2. Highlight artwork, statuary, collectibles, and plants with individual lighting arrangements.
3. Adequate reading lamps are a must.
4. Use recessed reflectorized lights to accent special room areas.
5. Be sure floor, table, and hanging fixtures have adequate shades to prevent glare.

Reflection Factors

Area	Range	Average	Average ratio	Extreme ratio
Ceiling	70-90%	80%	8	9
Wall	40-60%	50%	5	4
Floor	20-50%	35%	3.5	2
Desk Top	25-50%	38%	3.8	2.5

The exposed track lighting by Lightolier, above right, incorporates the individual shades as part of the decor. A downlight pattern is created by the positioning of the flexible fixtures. The art pieces on the walls are particularly emphasized by the downlighting.

Brightness Contrast Considerations

The brightness of an object or surface depends on two things — the intensity of light falling on it and the proportion of that light reflected in the direction of the eye. A white surface will have a much higher brightness than a dark surface receiving the same intensity of illumination.

A convenient method of comparing the brightness of two different colored surfaces under the same light conditions is to compare their *reflection factor*. For example, a light cream-colored ceiling might reflect 80 percent of the light and a dark brown wall reflect only 10 percent. The brightness contrast between the ceiling and wall is eight to one if they are lighted to the same intensity in footcandles.

Whether or not this brightness contrast is one the average person can be comfortable with is questionable when it is compared with the experience of qualified lighting specialists. Over many years these lighting professionals have found that generally the most desirable reflection factors for large areas in a room are as shown above.

Looking at the extreme ratios of reflection factors, it would seem that the lighting experts are telling us that the brightness of a ceiling should not be much more than twice that of the walls or four times that of the existing floorcovering.

The reflection factors of upholstery fabric, drapery materials, floorcoverings, wall and ceiling colors are very important considerations in planning your decorating scheme. Also, they cannot be disregarded in working out your lighting plan if you wish to end up with appropriate as well as comfortable brightness contrasts.

A footcandle meter can be used to determine the reflection factor of any surface by comparing the intensity of light falling on it with the amount of light bouncing back. First, place the meter on the surface with the dial facing the predominant light source in the room and make a note of the footcandle reading. Next, face the meter dial toward the same surface spot about 3 inches away so the meter does not cast a shadow. Then, move the meter slowly away from the surface until the dial reading is steady. Note this reading and figure what percent of the first reading it is. This percentage is the reflection factor of the surface.

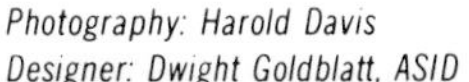
Photography: Harold Davis
Designer: Dwight Goldblatt, ASID

The living room above left is the same room as pictured on the opposite page, but this version shows the track lighting hidden. The baffle hiding the track system is easily painted or finished to provide a custom installation appearance.

Billiard and pool tables, such as the classic model above right, should have one 40-watt fluorescent fixture or two 150-watt or three 100-watt silver bowl reflector fixtures hung low over the table surface.

Family/Game Room Lighting

1. Plan adequate lighting to handle a variety of family activities.
2. Individual reading and desk lamps are required for comfortable and efficient use.
3. In a large family or game room, use lighting to define various activity areas.
4. Valance lighting and recessed ceiling fixtures are ideal for low-ceiling basement rooms.
5. Bridge and poker tables are best lit with four overhead reflector spotlights placed about 2 feet outside corners of game table.
6. Ping-pong tables should have a ceiling floodlight placed over each end of table.
7. Billiard and pool tables should have one 40-watt fluorescent fixture or two 150-watt or three 100-watt silver bowl reflector fixtures hung low over table surface.
8. Snack or bar area can use incandescent light to play up sparkling glassware. Lighted shelves or fluorescent fixture under front edge of bar are effective.

Surface Characteristics

Surface textures not only alter color appearance but also modify to some extent their apparent brightness. The highest brightness is reached when a light beam is reflected back to a viewer's eye from a polished or glossy surface. This is called *specular reflection*. Varying degrees of brightness result from diffuse reflection from matte or rough surfaces. Smooth "flat" paint surfaces will produce the highest brightness by diffuse reflection. The other extreme on the diffuse brightness scale might be that from coarse, nubby fabrics.

Textures of painted surfaces, wallpaper, drapes, upholstery fabrics, and floorcoverings, all affect your lighting plan and the selection of desirable brightness contrast. There will be practical compromises, of course, that favor the selection of relatively smooth surfaces for ease of maintenance.

Selecting Lighting Equipment

Any lighting equipment that is not totally concealed automatically becomes part of your decorating scheme. And, if concealed, the light rays given off that are evident on room surroundings as brightness

Photography: Harold Davis   Designer: Mary Ayers, ASID

Photography: Harold Davis   Designer: Whitney Chase

Chandeliers, such as the one above left, are the crowning glory of a tastefully decorated bedroom. There are many styles available, from the royal elegance of sparkling crystal to unique contemporary sculptures. No matter what style you choose, be sure you determine the size beforehand by taking into account the size of your furnishings.

From a decorating standpoint the portable lamps above right are in scale with the room furnishings. The bases and shades are compatible with the decorating scheme as a whole. The brightness of the lampshades should be within the limits of comfortable brightness contrast in the room.

areas are also part of your decor.

From a decorating standpoint, portable lamps should be in scale with room furnishings with bases and shades compatible with the color scheme of the area. The brightness of lampshades should be within the limits of comfortable brightness contrast in the room.

Fixtures for general lighting of an area, suspended or mounted on the ceiling, should be in scale with the room size and styled to fit into the decor. The brightness of exposed light sources or shades should be checked to avoid glare spots.

If lighting equipment is concealed in cornices, valances, or soffits, it should be truly hidden so it cannot be seen by anyone sitting or standing in the room. The light emitted from such concealed equipment should not produce excessively bright areas in a room.

One of the most common misuses of lighting equipment is bare-bulb candelabras in dining rooms and other spaces. Unless attention is given to the brightness of incandescent bulbs, they can produce an uncomfortable glare spot in any room. This type of glare or excessive brightness can be reduced to a comfortable level by the installation of a dimmer control in the area switch box.

What this all adds up to is that the lighting equipment available to anyone can be one of the most important elements in your decorating scheme. It should be evident by now that a well-designed lighting plan can put life and vitality into your home decorating scheme.

Choosing a Chandelier

When it comes to selecting lighting fixtures for the home, it's a well-known fact that people spend the most amount of time choosing a chandelier, generally for the dining area. Although chandeliers can enhance a foyer, family room, or bedroom as well, they are the crowning glory to a tastefully decorated dining room. There are many styles available, from the royal elegance of sparkling crystal to unique contemporary sculptures. No matter what style you choose, there are some factors you should consider before you buy.

1. How large should it be? What chandelier diameter is right for the size of the room? In general, if your dining area is less than 10′ wide, look

Photography: Harold Davis   Designer: Noel Birns, ASID

Photography: Harold Davis   Designer: Holmes Ely, ASID

For the look of luxurious bathing, nothing beats chandeliers in the bathroom, see above left. These striking features reflect a definite personal taste in decorating. The chandeliers operate independently of each other and the recessed ceiling fixtures. One chandelier is for general illumination, while the other highlights the dressing table area.

This old-fashioned chandelier with the flame-shaped components, above right, follows the few simple rules of size and scale for decorating. A 6" clearance from each side of the table is maintained, and the bottom is approximately 30" from the tabletop. Generally, a chandelier should neither overpower a dining room nor should it be dwarfed by the room.

for a chandelier with a diameter of about 24" or less. The styling of the chandelier can affect the size you select. Decorators refer to this as "scale" of the chandelier to the room. If it is a light, airy, open design, you can hang a 26" diameter chandelier in smaller rooms. If it is more full-bodied, a 25" diameter will scale to a larger room than general guidelines normally indicate.

You must also consider the size of your dining table. Maintain a 6" clearance from each side of the table, so your chandelier should be 12" narrower than the width of the table.

2. How high should it be? In most dining areas, the bottom of the chandelier should be approximately 30" above the table. This provides proper lighting while keeping the chandelier out of your line of sight when seated. If the ceiling is more than the usual 8' height, you may want to raise the chandelier a few inches to maintain a much better room scale.

3. What about outlets? If there's no ceiling outlet, or if one is not located where you want the chandelier, you can solve the problem. A swag kit will let you plug into a wall outlet, or swag the chandelier from an outlet box to a ceiling hook over the location you ultimately desire.

Mood Conditioning

If all the reports are true, the average homemaker likes to have the right atmosphere for each social occasion. To satisfy this desire, any home should be able to offer mood conditioning. This means that the atmosphere in any room used socially could be changed from "restful" to "exciting" with the flick of a switch or two. Or a space might change from "warm" to "cool" or "casual" to "businesslike" by the same means.

For example, many dining areas are lighted by a candelabra fixture equipped with small flame-shaped incandescent bulbs. Hanging over the center of the dining table, the fixture illuminates the table and room for all family meals. For a baked-beans-and-brown-bread, Saturday-night supper, this light alone, to full brightness, is enough. Everything that evening is informal, from food and table setting to dress.

But the Sunday night "company is coming" formal occasion has the table set with the best linens, china,

Photography: General Electric

Photography: Harold Davis
Designer: Martin Duncan, ASID of Cannell and Chaffin

The mood lighting inside the living room above left is enhanced by the attractive lighting outside. A swimming pool offers almost as much pleasure as an area to view and as a background for entertaining as it does in the swimming it provides—and this is especially true at night.

The very elaborate chandelier above right is ideal for such a formal dining room. Mood lighting changes the atmosphere of a room such as this by the addition of lighted candles and a turn of the dimmer control switch.

and silverware. Candlelight graces the table and the center candelabra lighting fixture bulbs are dimmed down to match the candle flames below and cast a warm glow throughout the room.

Mood lighting changes the atmosphere of a room easily by adding lighted candles and a quick turn of the dimming switch.

Dining Room Lighting

General

1. Keep visual emphasis off the ceilings and walls and on decor, guests, and food.
2. Valance perimeter lighting can be particularly effective in dining areas.
3. Modern settings can make use of luminous ceiling panels with translucent or diffuser grid panels.
4. Cornice, recessed downlights, and wall washers are popular with traditional decor.

Accent

1. Use dimmer controls on chandelier to regulate room atmosphere.
2. Ceiling downlights should focus primarily on dining room table surface.
3. Candles and fuel lamps in decorative holders add a special touch to any meal.
4. Buffet, service areas, and china or silverware displays deserve special lighting emphasis.

The rather basic lighting plan developed in Chapter 4 for a typical living room demonstrates the mood conditioning flexibility that can be built into any lighting system. For this evening occasion, guests have been invited to meet the family's daughter, who has just received her advance degree in music.

As the guests arrived, the living room lighting was established at medium intensity using the 3-way portable lamps around the room. This produced a soft general illumination conducive to good conversation. As the evening progressed, the daughter was prevailed upon to demonstrate her musical skills. The father quietly turned on the piano spotlights, the mother adjusted 3-way lamps to low to focus attention on the artist.

When the presentation was over,

Photography: Harold Davis Designers: Tom Irwin and Lil Chain, ASID

The very contemporary look of the living room/dining room combination above demands contemporary lighting fixtures. A very ornate crystal chandelier or an Early American lamp would look ridiculous here. These fixtures combine maximum efficiency with a styling that turns them into a decorating plus.

the party took on a gala mood. The piano spots were turned off and the rest of the lighting, including cornice lights, was turned on high to create a lively atmosphere.

Does this sound like stage lighting directions in a theatrical script? It truly is that, showing how you too can stage social occasions in your own home by including simple but effective mood lighting. Incidentally, the dimmer mentioned in the dining room story is a simple one that can replace your present wall switch. It can be purchased at almost any electrical supply shop for a few dollars and quickly installed by the average homeowner.

If the general illumination in a room comes mainly from fluorescent light sources, a change from warm to cool atmosphere involves a simple change of fluorescent tubes from Deluxe Warm White to Deluxe Cool White. Such a change is quite common in climates that may be extremely warm in the summer time. When the cooler season arrives, the "warm" tubes can be used again.

Photography: Western Wood Products Assn.

There are several reasons why kitchen lighting requires special consideration. One is that national statistics show that lights are used in the kitchen more than any other room—an average of 868 hours a year. Also, most accidents are due to poor lighting.

6 Light for Work

In this chapter we will be primarily concerned with efficient lighting—enough light of the appropriate quality, properly placed to make household duties easier and safer—as opposed to decorative and dramatic mood lighting discussed in other chapters. The specific design challenge is for good task lighting, with decorative aspects as a secondary concern.

As in any lighting plan, both general illumination and spotlighting must be considered. An overall glare-free light level makes working conditions much more pleasant and enjoyable. Poor lighting makes extra work of any job when you must fight the conditions as well as the specific task. Spotlighting or task lighting provides the extra illumination for close, detailed work without eye strain. A sound plan usually includes fixed lighting for general illumination plus spotlighting or portable lights to focus on specific work areas.

The subject of work lighting has more information available than any other area of home lighting. Both major lamp manufacturers and industry have invested the time and money necessary to thoroughly research this subject. From the research, specific lamps and fixtures have been designed to overcome problems or to meet certain job requirements. Much of this industrial illumination information can be translated directly into solutions for home work lighting needs.

Kitchen Lighting

If you analyze your home, you will probably find that your kitchen is the most thoroughly illuminated room in the house—and with good reason. Today's professional kitchen planners understand that a proper lighting system for this important room is much more than a light over the sink and one in the ceiling center.

Professionals often consider lighting the first priority design item after the basic floor plan has been established. The goal is to establish effective kitchen lighting so that the light sources are not apparent, but the individual work surfaces are sufficiently illuminated. Much research has been done on this area of the home, but a good lighting plan is still a difficult task to achieve.

Lighting a kitchen involves a number of factors not encountered in other rooms. Although a kitchen is one enclosed space, there are a number of different activities that take place within it—food preparation, cooking, serving, dining, and, finally, the cleanup chores necessary before the next meal.

To compound the problem, a kitchen offers a series of unique lighting situations from the dark corners of cabinets, pantries, and base cabinets beneath the countertops to the smooth, glossy appliance and counter surfaces that produce unwanted glare. For this reason, professional kitchen designers use every trick in the book—skylights, recessed fixtures, pendant lamps, and in-cabinet illumination—to successfully solve the problems.

Kitchen lighting usually makes use of three types of illumination. On sunny days windows may supply as much light as is needed for general illumination. Tranluscent curtains or blinds can be used to soften daylight

Photography: Harold Davis Designer: Catherine Armstrong, ASID

Photography: Harold Davis Designer: Edward C. Turrentine, ASID

It makes good sense to plan a kitchen with a central lighting fixture such as the luminous ceiling above left. An entirely luminous ceiling, while efficient, might be monotonous. A good compromise is partial luminosity in conjunction with recessed spots. The fact that the cabinets and countertops here are not stark white cuts down on glare.

The luminosity problem in the kitchen above right is solved by the small size of the kitchen. A smaller fixture might not provide adequate task lighting and might darken the room, making it seem even smaller. There is additional task lighting in work areas such as over the sink and stove.

glare. Incandescent lighting is sometimes used for both general and local brightness. When downlights are used, mount them close enough together so that their beams of light cross and minimize any distracting shadows on the work surfaces.

Kitchen Lighting Tips

1. Plan carefully on paper. Sketch out kitchen dimensions detailing major appliances, counters, islands, and natural light sources.
2. General lighting for a kitchen should be well distributed, uniform, and as shadowless as possible.
3. Fluorescent fixtures reduce energy demand without sacrificing illumination. Use diffusers to scatter shadows from corners. Shielded spotlights control contrast.
4. Even if you are fortunate enough to have a window, install downlighting over the sink for cloudy days or dark nights.
5. Consider building lighting into the hood over your range.
6. Kitchen table, counter bars, and other eating areas can use a separate light fixture. Adjustable pull-down units provide flexibility.
7. Special task lighting for key work areas can be installed in the ceiling or in upper cabinets.
8. Don't forget light for storage areas in pantry or wall cabinets. Overhead or shelf-mounted brackets will do the job.

Fluorescent lighting is now the most popular form of artificial illumination for kitchen use. The tubes last up to ten times longer than incandescent bulbs and produce three to four times as much light for the current used. Compared to bulbs, the tubes are much cooler, and this can be an important factor in a kitchen already heated by an oven or surface burners on the stove. Since the light source is considerably longer, the light is spread more evenly and less glare is produced. The slender tubes are ideally shaped for installation under cabinets and in valances or soffits.

For the best color balance, Natural White fluorescent is recommended to make food look natural and tasty. Deluxe Warm White or Standard Warm White can be used in kitchens with a warm color scheme or lots of

Photography: Westinghouse Electric

Avoid placing your primary light source in the middle of the kitchen ceiling. General illumination seldom provides all the light necessary for a comfortable and efficient kitchen. The kitchen above left shows how wood cabinetry can avoid the problem of glare in all-white kitchens.

One of the many uses of General Electric's Hi-Light, above right, is brightening kitchen work surfaces. The new decorative lighting fixture features GE's long-lasting, energy-efficient Bright Stik.

wood tones. Where cool colors are predominate, Deluxe Cool White tubes are preferred.

General Illumination

Avoid placing your primary light source in the middle of the kitchen ceiling. Since most of the counter work surfaces are arranged along the outside of the room, you will constantly be working in your own shadow. Instead, consider placing your ceiling illumination off-center to better conform to your various work areas. Fluorescent fixtures positioned in an L, U, or rectangular shape will provide better illumination and a more interesting pattern.

An alternate suggestion to bring light to the perimeter of the kitchen is to use a large luminous ceiling panel, usually 4 feet by 6 feet in size. The best but most expensive method is to install a full luminous ceiling where the entire surface becomes the light source. Fluorescent fixtures are mounted above a complete ceiling of translucent plastic to provide shadowless light to the entire kitchen.

Additional built-in general lighting includes recessed ceiling fixtures, light fixtures installed inside the soffit area, or indirect valance lighting mounted on the face of the soffit between cabinet tops and the ceiling. Where cabinets have no soffits above and are at least 12 inches from the ceiling, bare fluorescent channels can be placed on top of the cabinets and tilted at a 45-degree angle to throw light up toward the ceiling.

Local Lighting

General illumination seldom provides all the light necessary for a comfortable and efficient kitchen. Additional local light is needed to illuminate the individual work surfaces. Stainless steel and other highly polished surfaces often create an uncomfortable glare. Light-colored walls and a matte or semi-matte texture on the laminated countertop surface reflect the overhead light without causing glare.

The sink is one of the busiest spots in the kitchen. A greater variety of tasks requiring good visibility—scrubbing, peeling, and slicing vegetables, scraping dirty pots and dishes, etc.—are performed in this location. Good, shadow-free lighting is a must. To avoid working in one's own shadow, the light must fall on the area in front of the worker.

The simplest answer may be a

Photography: Westinghouse Electric

Photography: Harold Davis Designers: Jack Stevens and Reg Allen

General illumination in the kitchen above left is provided by a surface-mounted wood trim fixture that has four 20-watt deluxe warm white tubes. A continuous strip of fluorescent lighting is used under the cabinets to light countertops and sink area. A white ceiling, walls, and countertop, and an off-white floor compensate for the light-absorbing qualities of the wood cabinets.

For sink areas up to 36 inches wide, such as the kitchen above right, two surface-mounted or recessed incandescent downlights with 75-watt reflector bulbs are recommended. Wider areas, up to 48 inches, will need three fixtures.

surface-mounted glass drum fixture centered over the sink with a minimum of 100 watts of illumination. A more efficient plan, where there is a soffit over the sink, is to recess fluorescent or incandescent fixtures. A two-tube shielded fluorescent fixture with Natural White tubes should extend the full width of the space between side cabinets. An unshielded fluorescent channel can be used in the hollow space, but the interior should be painted a matte white for improved lighting.

For sink areas up to 36 inches wide, two surface-mounted or recessed incandescent downlights with 75-watt reflector bulbs are recommended. Wider areas, up to 48 inches, will need three fixtures. For sinks under shallow cabinets overhead, fluorescent tubes are usually mounted on the cabinet bottom with a decorative valance to soften the potential glare.

Range units also demand adequate lighting. Some come equipped with a range hood with a single 100-watt or two 60-watt bulbs. Where there is no hood over a range unit located against a kitchen wall, a fluorescent fixture, at least 36 inches long and mounted 58 inches above the floor is recommended. Where high cabinets are above the range, you can use a built-in valance bracket with a fluorescent fixture, or a shelf with a light below for illumination and spice or cookbook storage. Freestanding ranges without a hood can use a large ceiling-mounted fixture or several recessed downlights with 75-watt reflector bulbs.

Work surfaces and countertops need a local light source for areas 3 feet or longer. Ideally, fluorescent lamps should run the full length of the work area. However, a 20-watt tube in a space up to 36 inches, a 30-watt tube up to 48 inches, and a 40-watt tube up to 60 inches will provide sufficient light. A number of undercabinet tubes are now available in standard sizes, and some very shallow 1-inch fixtures that are inconspicuous do a good job.

Island counters and dining areas can be treated similarly. Recessed ceiling downlights, large hanging fixtures, or adjustable pendant fixtures at least 72 inches from the floor can be used. In the dining area multilevel switches or dimmer controls alllow you to adapt the lighting atmosphere for a teenage party or a late night snack.

Photography: Harold Davis Designer: Wendy Zupner

Photography: Harold Davis Designer: Holmes Ely, ASID

The most critical area in a bath like the one above left is around the mirror. This is basic for good grooming. For shaving, makeup application, and hair care, the light should be soft and diffused, without glare or shadow.

Many larger-sized baths with sectionalized areas such as in the photo above right benefit from several overhead fixtures. These are generally recessed into the ceiling, and those over a tub or shower must be watertight and vaporproof.

Bath Lighting

For a relatively small room, the bath area can use a number of different types of lighting. General lighting is necessary, and in a compact bath, a central ceiling fixture may suffice. Medium and larger size baths, and especially those with sectionalized areas for tub/shower and toilet, will require several overhead fixtures. These are generally recessed into the ceiling, and those over a tub or shower must be watertight and vaporproof. A minimum of 100-watt incandescent or 60-watt fluorescent lamps is sufficient.

The most critical lighting in a bath centers around the mirror area. This is basic for good grooming. For shaving, makeup application, and hair care, the light should be soft and diffused, without glare or shadow. The face should be lighted from above and from both sides. Avoid lighting the mirror itself, rather light the face of the person looking into the mirror.

The most efficient method to light a person is to use three fixtures, one on either side of the mirror and one overhead. Side fixtures should be mounted 30 to 36 inches apart on the wall and installed about 60 inches above the floor. An overhead ceiling fixture should be centered over the front edge of the wash bowl. Incandescent fixtures should have a minimum of 75-watt bulbs and fluorescent tubes on the sides should be 20-watt or larger with one 30-watt or two 15-watt fixtures overhead.

For a theatrical touch to your bath, consider mounting incandescent strip fixtures around three or four sides of the mirror. The lights are 25-watt frosted or globe-shaped bulbs in decorative reflectors mounted on metal strips.

Additional bath lighting for specific purposes may include plant lights to take advantage of bath humidity for growing both flowers and ferns. A pedicure light, installed under the bowl or counter, provides illumination for foot beauty care. Here, an eyeball fixture or hooded bullet with a 75-watt reflector bulb does the trick.

Ceiling-installed infrared heat lamps can be used to warm the bath area in the spring and fall when regular house heating may not be operating. They also provide comfort when you step from the tub or keep a baby warm while drying and dressing. For a healthy year-round tan, sun

Photography: Montgomery Ward

Photography: Montgomery Ward

The luxurious master bedroom suite above left is one of the most dramatic features of a restored brownstone. For the private sleeping area, the designers devoted the narrow inner room to a stunning fabric-tented bed. Soft, nostalgic balloon-shade window treatments, pin-up bed lamps, a pedestal nightstand, and a slender "salt box" armoire complete the scene.

In selecting table lamps for the main living area above right, the designers made certain that the lamps were not the focus of attention. They are instead an attractive adjunct to the total look of the room.

lamps may be recessed into the ceiling or mounted on either side of the mirror. Ozone lamps help keep bathroom air fresh and pleasant. Always install them above eye level in a shielded metal fixture. Finally, for convenience or safety with small children, a small 7-watt incandescent plug-in night-light or an illuminated switch plate, which serves as both night-light and switch locator in a darkened bathroom, can be added.

Reading Lights

For maximum pleasure from reading and for easier concentration, reading lamps must have the proper quality and quantity of illumination and be placed so that the light falls comfortably on the open page. Reading light arrangements are flexible enough to fit any decorating scheme, but careful placement of the light source is critical.

Floor lamps used as reading lights should be 40 to 49 inches from the floor to the bottom edge of the shade. The shade should be moderately luminous to softly diffuse the light and eliminate glare. Open-top shades are preferred. If the floor lamp has a table around the shaft, the square or round table should be no more than 12 inches in diameter so the lamp may be placed close enough to the reading chair.

Floor lamps should use a 150- or 200-watt incandescent bulb, or for better lighting and mood control, a 3-way bulb of at least 200-watt capacity. Place low floor lamps in line with the shoulders when seated, and for taller lamps, place 15 inches left or right of the book center and 26 inches back from this spot.

All table lamps for reading should have the bottom edge of the shade at eye level as you sit in the chair, approximately 40 inches from the floor. Since table heights may vary from 18 to 26 inches from the floor, it is necessary to make sure that the combined height of the table plus the lamp base add up to the 40-inch height at shade bottom from the floor. Where the shade is too low, the lamp must be moved uncomfortably close to the reader; when the shade is above eye level, the reader can look up into the glare within the lamp shade.

Shades should be moderately luminous, with open-top models preferred. Dimensions may be 16 to 18 inches across the bottom, either straight or tapered sides, and a

Photography: Harold Davis Designers: Tom Quaggin and Tom Hadley

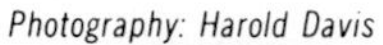
Photography: Harold Davis

The reading lamps in this teenager's bedroom, above left, take their design key from the room's decor. The unusual overhead lamp in the shape of a construction pipe is functional, yet amusing. The room was decorated by Whitney Chase Interiors.

The reading lamp in the living room above right fills the major requirements for good visibility. The bottom edge of the shade is at eye level for a person sitting on the couch. Where the shade is too low, the lamp must be moved uncomfortably close to the reader. Where it is above eye level, the reader can be bothered by glare.

height between 10 and 20 inches, depending on the lamp style and table height from the floor.

Table reading lamps should be positioned in line with the reader's shoulder, 20 inches to the left or right of book center. Soft White incandescent 150- or 200-watt bulbs or 3-way 50/200- or 100/300-watt bulbs will supply adequate illumination. For wattages of 200 and above, diffusers are recommended. For reading in bed, the sizes and lamp position for floor and table lights hold true for the bedroom as for other areas in the home. Some headboards have built-in lighting or small clip-on lights may be used if the wattage is sufficient. Single beds can use a 36-inch fluorescent fixture mounted on the wall about 30 inches above the mattress. Double beds need a 48-inch tube, and king-size or twin beds, a pair of 36- or 48-inch fluorescent tubes. The shielding material to hide the fixture and channel the light is usually opaque or semitranslucent material.

Desk Lighting

Desks may serve a variety of functions in the average home—casual correspondence, bill paying, teenage study center, income tax preparation, or the serious job of writing the great American novel. Yet, with all this diversity, the lighting principles remain the same. In general, desk lighting should be uniform, shadow- and glare-free, comfortable, and properly positioned for right- or left-handed individuals. A minimum illumination level of 200 watts of incandescent or 40 watts of fluorescent light is recommended.

Desks should be placed against a wall in a quiet area of the home. Avoid placing them in front of windows, since daytime glare or nighttime darkness both cause distracting contrasts with reading and writing materials. Walls should be nonglossy and free of distracting wallpaper patterns. The desk surface should be light in color and nonglossy for best results. A large, light-colored blotter or writing surface can be added to a traditionally dark finished wood desk surface.

A table lamp used on the desk should have the lower edge of the shade approximately 15 inches above the desk surfaces—about eye level for the average adult. The shade can be light in color, open at the top, and made of white or near-white material.

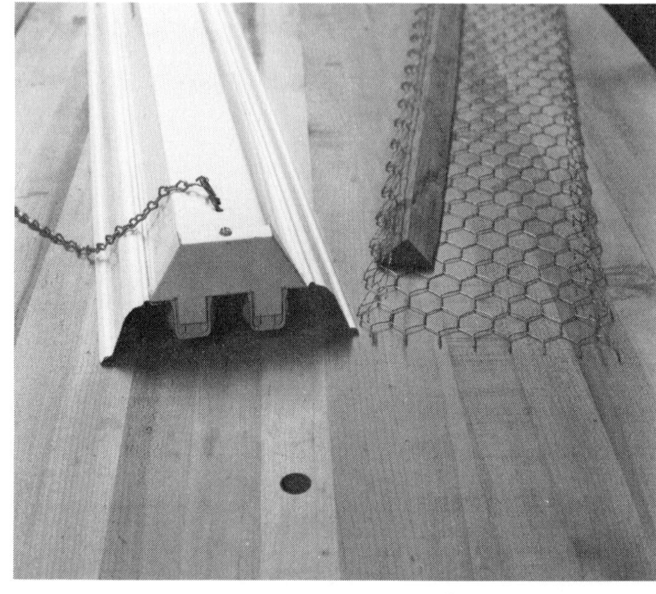

The adjustable angle lamp, like the one above left, was originally designed for use by architects on their drafting boards. It makes an ideal desk lamp for anyone. Springs on the arm counterbalance the lamp so that it may be clamped or screwed to the desk surface or wall for precise light placement.

A 200-watt frosted or Soft White 50/250, 3-way incandescent bulb is adequate. The center of the table lamp should be 15 inches to the left of the work center (or to the right for a left-handed person). The lamp should be a foot or so in from the front edge of the desk.

A fluorescent lighted shelf, mounted on the wall over the desk, is both efficient and practical. The shelf can hold reference books or store writing materials. Tubes should be 30- or 40-watt Deluxe Warm White and the fixture mounted 15 to 18 inches from the desk top to shelf bottom, and 12 inches from the front edge of the desk.

The adjustable angle lamp, originally designed for use by architects on their drafting boards, makes an ideal desk lamp. Springs on the arms counterbalance the lamp so that it may be clamped or screwed to the desk surface or wall for precise light placement. A 75- or 100-watt incandescent bulb with the reflective shade interior, concentrates the light with the effect of a larger bulb.

For small desk surfaces, the newest and most convenient light source is fluorescent strip lighting. The 25-inch unit needs no fixture or special wiring. The 33-watt fluorescent tube has a long life—up to five years in normal household use—and can be added wherever light is needed.

Workshop Lighting

In laying out a workshop, the power and light sources should be planned together. However, if at all possible, use separate circuits. The only thing worse than running your power saw blade into a hard knot in a board and blowing a fuse is running the blade into a knot, blowing a fuse, and finding yourself in the dark. Keep all the lighting on one circuit and power outlets on a second.

For general workshop lighting, the low-cost industrial fluorescent fixture with two 40-watt lamps is the best answer. The fixture comes with its own reflector and can be mounted directly on the outlet box or suspended by chains from hooks in the overhead rafters or floor joists. Position the fixture directly over the front edge of the workbench for maximum shadow-free illumination of the work surface. The tubes should be about 48 inches above the surface or 7½ to 8 feet off the floor.

This is the optimum height for best illumination; however, it can be

Photography: Bill Rooney

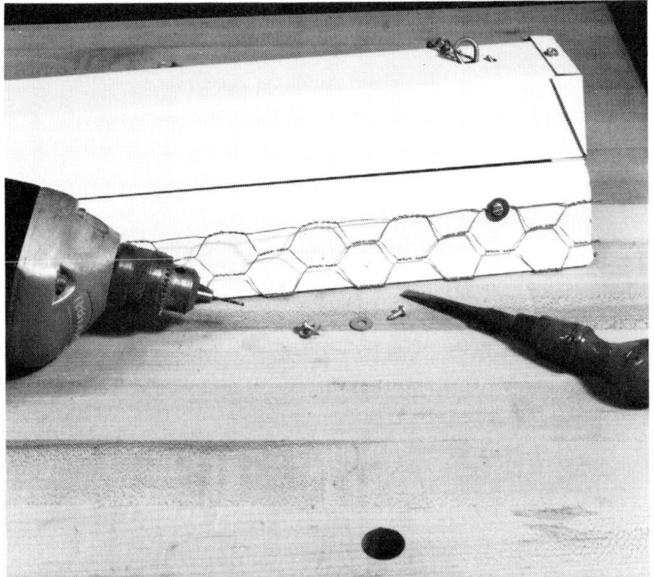

It's an easy job to safeguard workshop lights in the manner shown above. Cut a section of 1-inch wire mesh to the length of the fixture, 3 or 4 inches wider than the width across the reflector. Bend each long side of the mesh up 1½ to 2 inches using a board cut at a 45-degree angle. Holes 1/16 inch are drilled approximately 12 inches apart along the lower edge of the reflector, and the mesh is fastened into place using small sheet metal screws and washers.

uncomfortably low when working with long lengths of material. To prevent tube damage when handling oversize panels or long material, install protective wire screening along the bottom of the fixture. Cut a section of 1-inch wire mesh to the length of the fixture and 3 to 4 inches wider than the width across the reflector. Bend each long side of the mesh up 1½ to 2 inches using a board cut at a 45-degree angle. Holes 1/16 inch are drilled approximately 12 inches apart along the lower edge of the reflector, and the mesh is fastened into place using small sheet metal screws and washers. For a dollar or two and a few minutes work, your fixture tubes are protected from damage and the open mesh allows the full intensity of the light to shine through.

Bare incandescent bulbs should not be used in a shop. Put a good white reflector on them and the bulb will provide nearly twice as much light. Although fluorescent fixtures are the least expensive and most efficient lighting for a home shop, there is one location where they should *not* be used. A wood-turning lathe as it rotates the stock between centers sets up a disturbing set of false visual images if the lathe speed and the arcing speed of the fluorescent tubes overhead are in syncopation. Avoid this potential danger by using an incandescent fixture over the lathe.

Some portable power tools—sabre saws, routers—and stationary tools—drill presses, grinders, band saws—have lighting built into the equipment. For those that don't or for other low light jobs, low cost clip-on spotlights with reflector shields are handy. A 75-watt bulb is usually plenty of light.

Is there a special light for the home workshop? You bet there is, and it's a light tool. The portable torch lamp uses a 600-watt quartz-bromide lamp bulb to generate 800 degrees worth of concentrated heat. The torch lamp is used to remove paint and varnish when held 10 inches from the surface. The finish blisters, softens, and can be removed with a putty knife or wire brush. The heat torch can soften vinyl and asphalt floor tile, remove tiles by softening the mastic, and heat plastic laminate edging for easy bending. It dries glue, paint samples, and is the safest method for thawing frozen water pipes and locks.

7 Gallery of Lighting Ideas

Color and light go hand in hand. Separately, they are only tools, but together, light plus color can generate magic. This chapter should prove particularly helpful in planning your lighting systems and designing both interior and exterior settings for a new home or a personalized remodeling project.

The fascinating thing about lighting today is its ability to answer every type of need and decorating taste. By carefully blending natural light sources with the individual properties of incandescent and fluorescent lighting, you can create or change a wide range of moods. Manufacturers make available a size and shape light fixture to meet any situation. The selection is abundant.

Before you begin fixture selection, it is necessary to determine the psychological and technical requirements for an area in your home. The lifestyle analysis and the determination of light levels needed to satisfy certain seeing tasks must be completed first. Once these are done, your parameters are established, and the fixture selection becomes a matter of individual taste and budget considerations.

As photos in this book illustrate, the fixture, in some cases, may be the star of the room. A number of striking and highly individual light fixtures are now available that deserve visual attention. These "light sculptures" are not inexpensive, but they are handsome and practical additions to any room setting. The less conventional looking they are, the more careful you must be in using them, but the dramatic results are well worth the time and care taken.

In other instances, the light source is recessed or hidden from view. Here, the lighting effect rather than the fixture dominates the setting. Valances, cove lighting, and luminous ceilings on the interior, and landscape or architectural lighting on the exterior are used to create certain moods or a special atmosphere without drawing attention to the specific light source.

Technical Information

Throughout this book are sections containing facts, information, charts, and ratios covering various technical aspects of light and lighting applications. Although these may not be the most exciting sections, they are important.

Unless you fully understand light, glare, the interrelationship of light and color, and the effect of surface texture, your decorating plans may be dissappointing. Without a knowledge of light levels and how to measure them, or the benefits of reflectance values in natural and artificial lighting situations, you run the risk of either under-illuminating a key area or providing too much light, which is unnecessarily expensive.

The book is crammed with ideas, suggestions, both decorative and practical. Review them carefully, adopt the best ones to fit your family's needs, and then add to and improve upon them. We've tried to supply an idea file and working tool to answer your immediate needs and to provide a resource to solve future problems. One bright idea, we've found, often generates additional concepts. Flick the creative switch.

Paneling applied at an angle leads the eye upward to the roof skylight and the four amber glass, flame bulb chandeliers hanging over the stairway. Wall-mounted fixtures and recessed ceiling spotlights provide practical illumination to the interior.

Photography: Idaka
Architects: Schwab and Twitty

Photography: Bob Strode

Fluorescent Practical Beauty

There was a day when fluorescent lighting was confined to industrial illumination only. It was accepted as a highly efficient light source, but most families would never consider "factory lighting" in their homes.

But all that is changing, and to help speed the acceptance of fluorescent lighting in the home for both decorative and practical reasons, General Electric Company designers developed the lighting system for a contemporary passive solar house called "The Sun House."

The living room, shown above, features a continuous luminous ceiling with 40-watt fluorescent tubes. The panels are of wood and cane construction to provide uniform casual lighting. Drop-in panels are easily removed when tube replacement is required. Above the overstuffed modular seating sections along two walls, simple brackets hide more 40-watt tubes. The wall brackets direct the light upward for a dramatic ceiling and wall effect, but also downward to serve as reading illumination on the sofa.

The electrical system was wired to allow wall and ceiling fixtures to be used separately or together depending on the activity. Light-colored interior surfaces improve the efficiency while providing a backdrop to accent the straw fan and coolie hat collection. Bright pillows add color-notes to a monochromatic decorating scheme.

The linear shape of fluorescent tubes fits naturally into wall brackets, soffits, ceiling coves, window cornices, and luminous ceiling panels. When planning for this type of built-in architectural lighting, the light source should be as unobtrusive as possible. The focus should be on the light effect and not on the fixture. In this manner, the lighting seems to be a natural part of the space, just as sunlight is during the daylight hours. The room is comfortably illuminated without looking staged.

While fluorescent lighting may look good, just how efficient is it? According to General Electric engineers, the lighting system for The Sun House cut the cost of electricity used for lighting alone by 63 percent with the almost exclusive use of fluorescent tubes instead of the typical incandescent household light bulbs. In hard dollars-and-cents terms, there was an estimated savings of $135.39 per year, based

on the national average energy rate of 3.7 cents per kilowatt hour.

The heart of the Sun House is a 432-square-foot solarium, which traps and stores the direct heat of the sun in the brick floor. The two-story glass-walled room runs the full length of the south-facing rear of the house and may be opened to the kitchen, dining and living rooms through the insulated sliding glass doors. During the day, the area is filled with natural sunlight and the designers provided for the same airy and open feeling at night. A pair of 30-watt fluorescent lamps are recessed into the four false beams spanning the room.

Additional lighting for a work/storage area at the rear of the room is provided by a 40-watt fluorescent tube over the sink hidden by a wall bracket. Several decorative kites suspended from the ceiling each contain a standard 40-watt incandescent bulb.

To help control both sunlight and glare during the day and to assure privacy in the evening, the upper section of the two-story outside wall is equipped with fabric roller shades while the lower portion uses narrow venetian blinds to regulate the light.

The secret to the success of the Sun House is illustrated in the photo above looking into the dining area. You are aware of light, but not the light sources. Here the luminous ceiling panels, on separate controls, have been dimmed to accent the fluorescent wall lighting hidden behind the hardwood bracket.

Fluorescent lighting differs from incandescent in two important ways—in color and in pattern. Most people are familiar with the difference in color effect when fluorescent light strikes surfaces, materials, or the skin and clothing of people. Part of this look comes from the difference in the light pattern. Fluorescent lighting is more diffuse, like the light from a slightly overcast sky or the illumination on a hazy day, which gives an even, overall, shadowless light in any space.

Because of its linear nature, fluorescent lamps can be used decoratively and dramatically to "wash" a whole wall with light. The most pleasant, warmest fluorescent tube for home lighting is Deluxe Warm White. Most people are comfortable and look healthier under it. There are those who prefer Deluxe Cool White tubes if their homes are in warm climates.

Photography: Steve Marley

Kitchen Collaborators

The kitchen is the busiest room in any home. When you add up the construction or remodeling costs per square foot plus the expense of stock or custom cabinetry and the cost of the various major and minor appliances, it is also the most expensive room.

As any woman will explain, if the kitchen is practical, pleasant, and workable, she is willing to put up with a number of shortcomings in other areas of the home. But a functional kitchen is vital. For this reason, many homeowners invest in the talents of professional designers and decorators to assure a successful kitchen project.

The kitchen illustrated in the three photos here is a good example of the results of collaborating with an experienced professional kitchen specialist. Designer Sarah Lee Roberts began this kitchen remodeling project with a thorough investigation. "I listen to all the homeowner's comments about her present kitchen before beginning to plan a new one. I also try to involve the whole family—anyone who's concerned with cooking. I listen carefully to everything that's said—what they want in a new kitchen, what annoys them about their present one.

"I ask about natural lighting changes that occur during the day that affect the mood and temperature of the space. I query them about their individual preferences, the specific equipment they want installed, and the overall look or style they prefer."

Once all the facts have been gathered and the budget established, the design work can begin. In this case, a light-filled kitchen with lots of space was requested. The homeowners also specified a durable, easy-care room with oak cabinets and floor compatible with the vintage period of the home. Since storage was somewhat limited, the designer added a stainless steel storage island with butcherblock work surface.

The lighting? Recessed and unobtrusive fixtures were used throughout. Spotlight, canister, track-mounted fixtures were hidden partially behind the overhead ceiling beams. The range hood contained built-in lighting. Hanging copper fixtures with swivel heads directed light onto the cooking utensil display over the sink area. A hanging brass

lamp with white globe softly diffused light over the dining table.

To contrast with the dark wood floors, cabinets, and overhead beams, walls, ceiling, and areas over the work surfaces were painted white or had light-colored, imported, Portuguese tile installed.

Natural light was introduced into the kitchen with a roof skylight using a diffusing translucent panel. A wall opposite the cooking area was opened up via picture windows, thereby enhancing the dining pleasure of those in the breakfast nook. A minimum of fixtures but maximum lighting efficiency.

"Good lighting," emphasizes designer Sarah Lee Roberts, "is absolutely vital to a well-planned, totally functional kitchen. We've lived too long with the center light for kitchen illumination—forever working in a shadow. I always plan for good general lighting plus task and mood lighting. I use dimmers extensively, and unobtrusive light sources such as recessed and under-cabinet lights, plus one decorative chandelier, if desired, installed over a dining table or a work island."

Today, kitchen specialists are changing their attitudes toward design projects. Years ago, they were fairly rigid about what constituted a good workable kitchen. Design began with the proper work triangle. The refrigerator was placed alongside the sink with appropriate counterspace nearby. Today, the mechanical aspects are no longer as important as having the homemaker happy with her kitchen. She may have to walk a few extra steps, but if the arrangement pleases her, then it's a good design.

Lighting is usually the first consideration after the basic floor plan has been developed. Natural light is used wherever possible, which means skylights or greenhouse windows, which let in light, and, when hung with plants, can be used to blot out an ugly view. The goal for artificial lighting is to come as close as possible to the natural effect. Surface fixtures are kept to a minimum because the light is too bright and produces dark corners. Instead, recessed fixtures with dimmer switches are preferred.
Says Roberts, "Make it your kitchen, not just space for some nebulous future home buyer. It's often those personal touches that ultimately help to sell a house to an interested buyer."

Photography: Karl Riek

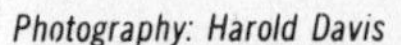

Photography: Harold Davis

Airy Kitchen

Shown above is a well-designed kitchen that takes full advantage of both architectural and natural lighting opportunities. A skylight installed in the steeply pitched roof over the sink area captures natural daylight. Below, the three-sectioned picture window allows full enjoyment of the terrace and backyard landscaping. The small window to the right of the sink cranks open for ventilation and also serves as a food pass-through when entertaining friends on the terrace.

Artificial lighting combines both fluorescent and incandescent fixtures. The display board, featuring the collection of decorative blue plates, hides fluorescent strip lighting behind for nighttime illumination of the busy sink area. Smaller fluorescent fixtures installed under the cabinets light the countertop work surfaces.

Suspended over the dining table is a white wood framework, which supports the hanging cooking utensils and four-sided track lighting electrified channels. Adjustable incandescent spotlights are focused on the work and dining areas to aid in household duties.

Country Kitchen

A California kitchen designed by Mary Fisher uses a variety of natural materials and textures to their best advantage. Dark natural woods in the cabinetry and floor are balanced by the rugged brick in the wall and arch over the range. Sand-colored glazed tiles on the island sink top, work surfaces, and range arch provide visual contrast and an easily maintained surface.

The vaulted white ceiling features recessed narrow skylights for daytime illumination, and incandescent spotlights in the ceiling are directed to the sink and informal eating bar.

This professionally designed kitchen is a real step-saver with a surprisingly compact work triangle. Food preparation, cooking, and serving are all within arm's reach of the homemaker.

Two pull-out maple breadboards are recessed into the base cabinet to the right of the range, and the maple snack bar surface doubles as a chopping board when preparing vegetables at the sink. Note the fluorescent light fixture hidden below the overhanging maple top.

Colorful fruit in hanging wire mesh baskets add decoration.

Photography: Idaka

Photography: General Electric Co.

Contemporary Kitchen

It's warm and interesting and exciting, and at the same time restful. It's contemporary, yet has a number of traditional touches. It borrows from a number of decorating styles, but the end result is an undefined yet very personal look.

What organizes all these differing elements into a successful working unit is the lighting design. The fanciful curved and peaked custom skylight with translucent panels supplies a soft, even, shadowless illumination to the kitchen and family room area. Mosaiclike stained glass window panes over the sink filter warm, natural light into the kitchen.

Overhead in the soffit above the window, recessed wall washers highlight the mahogany grain in the paneling while illuminating the work area. To the left, another set of recessed ceiling fixtures accent the warm copper tones of the range hood. Suspended beneath the hood, copper lights focus on food preparation and cooking activities.

Along the side wall, a marble slab with lighting in the soffit overhead serves as a handy desk area for casual correspondence or sorting of the monthly bills.

Light Wall

Architects and designers are beginning to realize that properly planned lighting schemes can do much more than simply illuminate an area. Light can be used to lead the eye toward certain features and away from less interesting elements in a room setting.

Light can "stage" a room or lead people through a home in the best traffic patterns. It can also create subtle barriers, visual walls instead of physical walls.

The photo above right illustrates lighting used as a room divider. A deep walnut light box at the ceiling contains fluorescent fixtures with a softening translucent panel below that illuminates the plants and flowers in the floor-level garden.

As the use of plants, shrubs, and flowers grows for interior design, proper lighting becomes more important. Sometimes standard light fixtures are used to accent the greenery, but there is a growing trend toward incandescent, fluorescent, or a combination of both to supply the light energy needed for sound plant growth. Plant lights are available in a variety of sizes and shapes to supply this special illumination.

Photography: General Electric Co.

Photography: James Brett

Accented Entrance

The friendly warmth of the entryway shown above left is the result of a combination of welcoming light seen through the interior of the two-story modern house and several simple but well-placed exterior lights.

Bright lighting on the exterior is not necessary, in fact, is usually unwanted. Instead low-wattage lamps are used to define shapes, areas, and textures. Ideally, the light effect should be reflected from trees, shrubs, or walls.

For this starkly modern structure, inexpensive PAR 38 external floodlights were installed at ground level and directed upward along the front facade at a sharp angle to highlight the heavily textured brickwork. Most people are familiar with the interplay of sunlight and shadow during daylight hours, but this visual magic can be even more dramatic after dark.

A low-voltage light fixture is used to mark the driveway entrance, and this is a particularly thoughtful idea in northern climates where a sudden snowfall can obliterate familiar landmarks. Prewired, low-voltage lighting systems are now available for homeowner installation.

Illuminated Exterior

Your lighting plan should include more than just entryway and walk illumination for the exterior of your home. Good lighting can play an active part in expanding the livability of any home.

The two-story redwood home above takes full advantage of the patio running the length of the rear elevation. Fortunately, this home has the privacy of a rural setting to make use of extensive large glass areas to capture the surrounding view. The lighting plan was simple but effective. Four large weatherproof fixtures were installed 15 feet above the patio surface on the boxed wood columns. The light is directed downward to illuminate the patio activities and upward to be reflected off the light-colored, wide overhanging soffit.

Exterior lighting delivers more than just the obvious. In addition to expanding your outdoor living into the evening hours, it provides visual excitement for your interior space. Guests can enjoy the beauty of your landscape efforts while sharing a meal at your dining table. Back-lit shrubs and trees take on unusual dramatic effects when seen through patio doors in the evening.

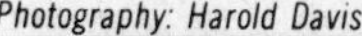

Photography: Harold Davis

Photography: Idaka

Climate Lighting

In the warmer sections of the country, designers must consider light, color, and temperature to create suitable interiors. The trick is to maximize the natural light source while restricting the glare and heat often accompanying the strong southern sun.

In the comfortably formal setting shown above, designer Barbara Lerner cleverly balanced the natural and artificial lighting for a controlled environment. A broad roof overhang outside the floor-to-ceiling glass walls reduced the direct impact of summer sunlight on the interior. Thin roll-up venetian blinds may be partially drawn or adjusted for glare-free viewing. Colorful drapes with reflector lining can be pulled to reduce direct light and heat.

Recessed incandescent fixtures in the redwood ceiling establish an unobtrusive but effective general room illumination level. The impressively grand cut-glass chandelier suspended over the dining table is wired with dimmer controls so that the flame-shaped bulbs can be dimmed to complement rather than compete with the candles on the table during formal dinner parties.

Done With Mirrors

If magicians and interior designers can do it, you too can use mirrors to fool the eye. As designer Ron Fidler proved in the dining area shown above, mirrors can make space seem larger. The relatively low ceiling appears to soar to new heights with the addition of mirrors over the dining table.

The star of the show is the suspended chandelier with its double cluster of low-wattage bulbs on a dimmer encased in transparent amber globes. It's perfectly in keeping with the contemporary-style chairs and glass and plastic table. Muted colors in the fabric wall design and paint scheme help make this setting work well.

This bold use of mirrors could have been a disaster in the hands of an amateur. The wrong colors or too bright a light source could have turned this area into a reflected jumble of distorted glare. The reflective values of fabric, paints, and smooth surfaces can wreak havoc with careless planning. Mirrors will only multiply the problems.

Fortunately, the sure hand of a professional kept all elements under control for spectacular results.

Photography: Karl Riek

Watery Wonderland

There is a special excitement when light and water are teamed up in the right setting. The water acts as a living mirror to reflect and enhance the impact of exterior lighting treatments. A pool scene represents an adventure and opportunity to be capitalized upon.

The backyard patio and pool setting shown above uses both landscape and in-pool illumination to create an outstanding yet practical entertainment area for family enjoyment or guest entertaining. Architect Michael J. O'Hearn, Habitec, Inc., designed an L-shaped pool to fit the lot corner that included multitiered decking and a stone-faced cascading waterfall fed by a recirculating water pump.

Exterior spotlights were installed under the adjoining house eaves for general illumination of the backyard area. The featured corner design called for low-voltage lighting hidden behind landscape boulders and the decking to cast light on the steps' horizontal and vertical surfaces. Waterproof in-pool lamps were installed along the pool edges.

Along the back lot line, a redwood board fence and red cedar shake corner wall with a decorative trellis top supplied both a wind break and needed privacy for the pool setting.

Unless handled carefully, the combination of exterior electrical systems and water can be dangerous. This type installation is one the homeowner should delegate to an experienced contractor. The National Electric Code has specific requirements that must be conformed to for a safe installation. Regular-voltage or low-voltage PAR floodlights cannot be installed closer than 5 feet to a pool. Underwater pool lighting requires 12-volt lamps available in 300- to 500-watt sizes. A ground fault interrupter can help assure electrical safety.

Exterior light bulbs, which are exposed to rain, snow, and a wide range of temperatures, should be weatherproof and shatter-resistant. PAR bulbs are the safest choice, but regular indoor bulbs can be used if the fixture is approved for exterior installation and a clear or tinted shield is used to protect the bulb from the elements.

Prewired, low-voltage lighting systems and exterior wall or pole light kits are now available. Also you may want to consider a photo-electric eye or timer to regulate outdoor lights.

Photography: Harold Davis

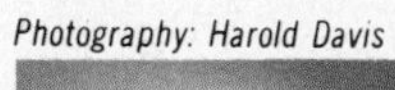

Photography: Harold Davis

Bold Bedroom

Simplicity is often the hallmark of good design. The professional decorator understands that "less" can actually be "more" when handled properly. A single outstanding element in a room can become the take-off point that sparks the tone for a room interior.

The huge bed with its unique raffia-wrapped treatment of the posts and overhead arches deserves to be placed on a raised carpeted pedestal. This handsome piece dominates the room, and all other items were selected to complement this central item. Colors, textures, and lighting take their direction from the bed.

Fluorescent fixtures in the deep ceiling box illuminate the striking blue, patterned, decorative panels and introduce a distinctly contrasting color to the room scheme. Tall, highly polished brass lamps on either side of the bed cast a warm incandescent glow and may be used for relaxed, bedtime reading.

Designers Kirsten Gaskill and Lynn Eastwood demonstrate the sure hand of professional understatement in treating this sleeping area with an unorthodox but highly successful decorating approach.

Dramatic Den

Designer Rita Barnett managed to blend a clear plexiglass modern desk with a traditional-styled green leather upholstered chair as if they were meant for each other. Then she added an oriental vase featured in a decidedly masculine rich wood storage console. Several sets of gold leaf, leather-bound books and statuary complete the oppulent atmosphere.

A small brass-base desk lamp provides illumination for the work surface. The crowning touch is found in the hidden fluorescent valance lighting throwing a soft blue-green cast on the light-colored ceiling and down onto the vase below. Metallic venetian blinds reflected in the vase mirror help control natural light glare in the late afternoon.

The den projects a strong personality of its own. Rich, natural, textured material abounds, and the designer cleverly echoed the green tones of the overhead lighting, lamp-shade, and chair upholstery in the carpeting and drapes.

In a relatively dark color scheme such as designed for this room, dimmers can help provide the exact light intensity required.

Photography: Steve Marley

Golden Arches

The process of adding on space to an existing home can take many forms. Architect Bart Prince was assigned the task of designing an adult entertainment space in a family room large enough to showcase a beautiful rug inherited by the proud homeowners.

The standard solution to this type of request is to make a ground floor addition to the present house. "But I didn't see a ground floor room. It would eat up too much valuable lot space," recalls Prince. "And I didn't see a rectangular room for that marvelous rug."

Prince's answer was nothing square, rectangular, or simple. His suggestion was a complex of curves hung in space. The second-story structure is suspended on four steel columns, which support the curving laminated wood ceiling beams. The gigantic custom-built beams were lifted in place by a crane. The twin circular elements, which house a closet and bath at the end of the room, add lateral support so that the addition does not sway in the wind.

Lighting was simplicity itself. Fan-shaped, floor-to-ceiling windows on both sides of the room provided abundant natural light during the daytime. The glassed-in circular stairway at the rear supplied additional daylight.

Artificial lighting suspended over the stairwell consisted of a spoke-shaped fixture with incandescent bulbs at the end of each arm. For the room interior, Prince recommended installation of incandescent globe bulbs along the bottom edge of the two massive laminated wood beams.

The lighting industry, architects, designers, and decorators are beginning to realize the full range of illuminating opportunities offered in residential lighting. For too long, most of their efforts have been directed toward solving problems in industrial and commercial settings. Now, however, architectural and design schools, realizing the interrelationship of artificial and natural light to color and texture, are incorporating this information into their classes.

Lighting manufacturers and fixture producers are introducing a variety of energy-saving lamps and a wide range of decorative fixtures. Wiring systems are being simplified so that the average homeowner can incorporate the advancements into his remodeling projects.

Photography: Saari & Foarri

Photography: General Electric

Redwood Remodel

When Catherine Ma, Minneapolis designer, accepted the challenge to remodel a multilevel condominium, the immediate problem was to change the rather sterile interior. Her response was to sheath the walls with a rich, warm redwood paneling.

A small area for before-dinner cocktails, shown above, was carved from the previous dining room and furnished with upholstered seating. The space was purposely kept dim, casual, and conversational. Tiny recessed pinlights outline the wall and ceiling beams.

A large brass pendant lamp was hung low enough over the glass table to eliminate direct glare for the seated guest. Through the redwood archway, fixtures hidden in the planter box backlight the greenery and play upward onto the closed window drapes.

A good lighting scheme need not be obvious and blatant. A subtle approach is usually much more effective and considerably easier to live with. Remember, this is your home, and there may be times you will have to say "no" to an architect or decorator if their ideas do not conform to your lifestyle.

Display Lighting

Part of the enjoyment of owning and collecting interesting objects is the opportunity to share your display with friends.

A basic light box, shown above, was installed behind a set of open shelves. The narrow frame, painted to blend with the surrounding wall, contains a series of translucent tubes behind a large sheet of translucent plastic. The uniform, shadow-free illumination shows off the glassware and figurines to their best advantage.

In the corner, a small fixture buried in the brass container creates a fanciful light pattern on the wall as it shines upward through the dried branches. It's an inexpensive but exciting lighting trick.

If you are looking for more display lighting ideas, a tour of your local art museum, historical society, galleries, and even display windows in retail stores will give you a look at how the professionals stagelight their objects. Overhead lighting and sidelighting can be effective to accent three dimensional items, backlighting, colored lights, display cases with glass or translucent plastic shelving lit from below, are all suggestions you can incorporate into your own display.

 Photography: Idaka

Globe Chandelier

The two photographs above illustrate dining areas with distinctive chandeliers. However, each has an entirely different atmosphere.

The dining room at the left was designed by the Childs-Dreyfus Group, Chicago, and a number of room elements contribute to the cool, stately decor. Cool colors in the ceiling, walls, and adjustable louver shutters, plus the blue window trim, seat cushions, and table napkins, visually reduce the temperature.

A generous use of glass in the tabletop, crystal goblets, and mirrored wall add to the clear, icy feeling. Even the low-wattage incandescent bulbs in the two-tiered globe chandelier contribute to the formal feeling. The normally warm light from the chandelier accents and passes through the glass surfaces rather than reflecting warm tones.

Hard, smooth, colorless surfaces can present a decorating problem unless they are handled with care. The red, glazed floor tile injects a little warmth into the setting, but it is the natural wood of the chairs and the Oriental rug beneath the table that allow this formal dining area to project a feeling of hospitality.

Tree Chandelier

Again, a dining area set for four. The furnishings and table setting are equally as formal as the adjoining photograph, but the overall feeling is entirely different.

The custom chandelier created by Garland Faulkner appears to be the root system for a tree growing in the floor above. It is a unique and fanciful fixture, yet it seems in perfect keeping with the room. Low-wattage pinpoint incandescent bulbs at the root tips collectively generate enough illumination for the table.

Along the upper portion of the rear wall, open wood grilles filter light from the hallway behind into the dining area. In this setting, the light has color to work with. The warm tones of the Oriental rug and soft beige walls, plus the natural wood in the table, chairs, and dark-stained oak stair trim, reflect a feeling of gracious hospitality.

It is interesting to note how the seating arrangement alone changes the tone. Chairs circling the table label this as a gathering, while pairs of chairs in the photo on the left project a more businesslike formal confrontation. Neither room is "better" than the other—just different.

Photography: General Electric

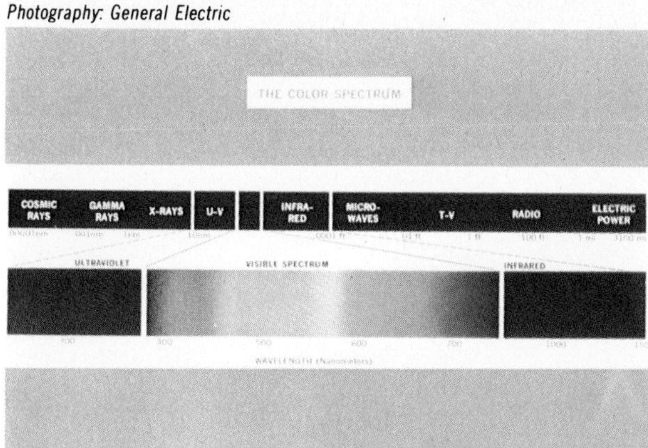

Fig. 1

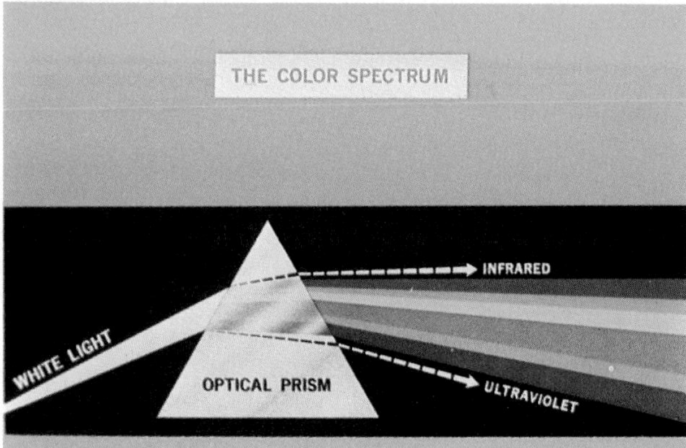

Fig. 2

Fig. 3

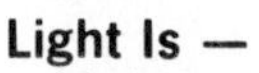

Light Is —

Light, as we have seen, is a variety of things when it comes to residential illumination. This final page of Chapter 7 contains photography borrowed from the General Electric technical brochure *Light and Color.*

Fig. 1 Light is much more than we can see with the naked eye. The sun and artificial lamps are light sources projecting radiant energy wavelengths. The shortest cycle of radiant energy is cosmic rays with a wavelength of 0.00001 nanometers. (One inch contains about 25.4 million nanometers.) At the other end of the known spectrum are electric power waves with an average length of 3,100 miles.

The spectrum of radiant energy waves we call "light" is very narrow, ranging from 380 to 760 nanometers. Immediately below the visible spectrum is ultraviolet energy, valuable for its germ-killing and suntanning properties. Below that are X-rays and gamma rays. Above the visible spectrum are infrared or heat rays followed by microwaves, TV, and radio waves.

Fig. 2 Light is color. "White light" is a relative balance of all visible wavelengths. A narrow beam of white light passed through a prism will spread and separate the individual wavelengths of visible energy so that the eye can distinguish between them. The normal eye will see three wide bands of blended color—violet, green, and red, with several narrower bands (blue, yellow, and orange) blended between the wider bands.

The color-blind eye will see only graduations of gray, or perhaps some of the colors and some gray (depending upon the extent of impairment of the eye).

Fig. 3 Light is color but color is light. The color booth illustrated above is used by lighting technicians and professional decorators for an accurate reading of various colors under differing light conditions. The picture shows two identical sets of color cards exposed to the same intensity but under lights of different tonal values. The identical cards do not look like the same colors to the naked eye.

We do not see the actual color inherent in a material, rather we interpret the light rays from a source reflected off the material surface back to our eye. This may seem like technical double-talk, but is a vitally important principle.

Photography: Harold Davis   Designer: Barbara Lerner

Lighting placement and the quality of lighting used in a bathroom contribute a lot to carefree grooming. The bathroom above gets an A+ in both categories. Strip lights surround the mirror providing shadow-free illumination. Good general lighting is attained from recessed ceiling lights.

8 Light for Beauty and Health

Most people are aware of the importance of light for growing healthy plants, but too often they fail to recognize how light affects the beauty and health of an individual. If you spent the day at the beach, you would see the visible light in the narrow spectrum falling between 375 and 760 nanometers. This is the same illumination we use indoors for grooming purposes—hair care, shaving, and makeup application.

While at the beach, you could not see, but would be aware of, two additional light energy sources. Just above the visible light spectrum you could feel the warmth generated by the infrared light rays. Immediately below the visible spectrum are the ultraviolet rays—the tanning, vitamin-giving, bacteria-killing, invisible rays.

Light for Grooming

Mirror lights in a bedroom or bath should provide shadow- and glare-free illumination. In grooming, the most critical task for a man is shaving, for a woman, applying makeup. A well-positioned mirror with carefully planned lighting can eliminate distracting shadows under the eyes, nose, cheeks, or chin. For best performance, makeup lighting should come from both sides of the mirror and from above. Side fixtures should be placed approximately 28 to 36 inches apart and centered about 5 feet off the floor. For full-face illumination, a fixture not less than 24 inches wide can be placed over the mirror approximately 78 inches off the floor.

Too often we have to make do with the grooming lighting in a home that we may inherit from the previous owner. If you are planning a new home or considering major remodeling, here is your opportunity to do it right. Consider using horizontal and vertical light strips mounted beside and above the mirror. Modern strip fixtures are available in chrome or satin brass-plated metal housing in four-bulb 29-inch lengths and six-bulb 41-inch sections. Strip lights may be joined end-to-end for long lengths or, using right-angle corners, installed in a square around all four sides of the mirror or U-shaped on three sides only. The result is a Broadway or Las Vegas showgirl dressing-room look.

For a more contemporary appearance, fluorescent strips or globe bulb incandescent units may be used to surround the makeup mirror. Three-sided mirrors, where the two side wings fold forward, usually require overhead ceiling fixtures that shed the light downward. Because of the shadows on the lower part of the face, this is usually not a satisfactory plan unless additional side lighting is employed to even out the lighting.

The quality of light is as important as the type and placement of fixtures when planning a grooming area. Incandescent soft white bulbs or deluxe warm white fluorescent tubes should be used for the most natural and flattering lighting. Individual light units should have 60- or 75-watt bulbs for sufficient illumination, but where multiple-bulb strip lights are used, 25- or 40-watt bulbs may be installed according to the manufacturer's recommendation.

In a dressing room or bedroom makeup table, table lamps are often

Illustration source: Lightolier

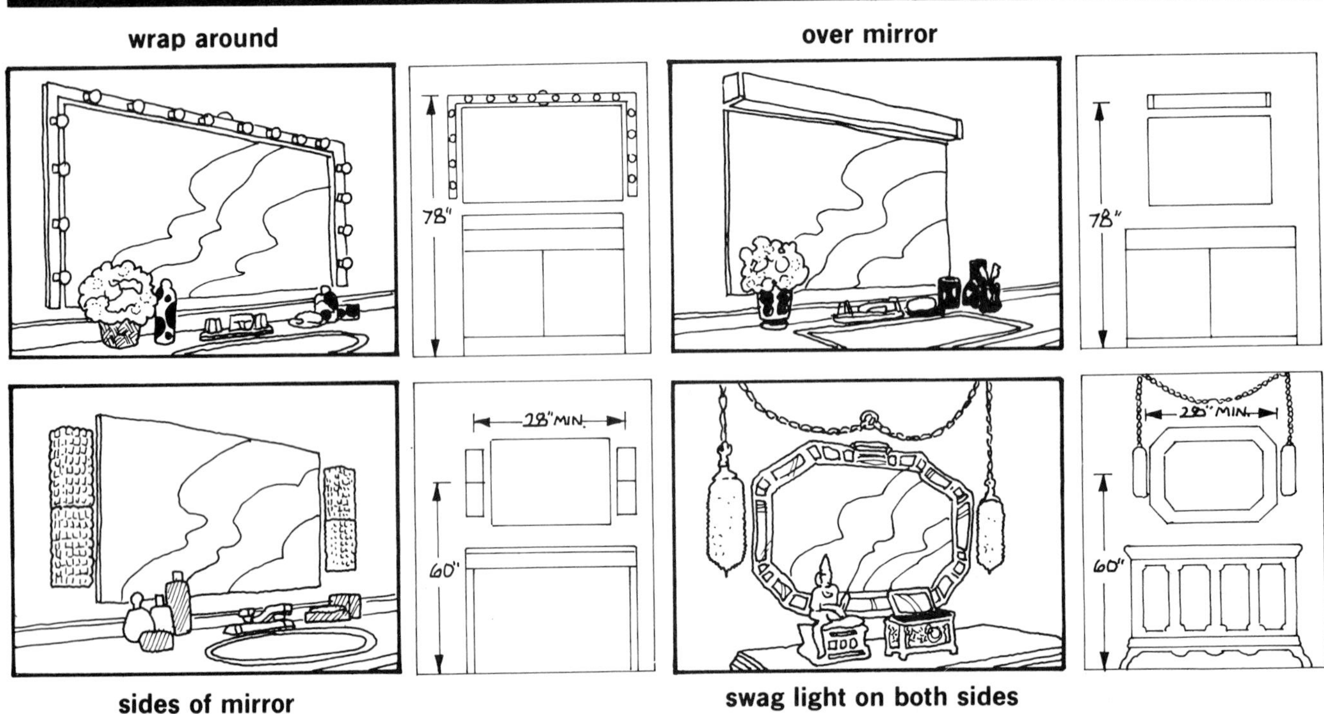

Good grooming requires shadow-free lighting for the important seeing tasks of shaving and applying makeup. There are many ways to do this. Illustrated above are a few examples of how to achieve good bath lighting.

used on either side of the mirror. White or off-white shades will prevent distortion of complexion color, and they should be centered about 36 inches apart and from 15 to 22 inches above the dressing table surface. The preferred bulbs are 100-watt soft-white or 30/100-watt 3-way bulbs in each shade.

Don't overlook the need for a mirror near the front door so that you may make a final necktie adjustment or pat a stray curl back into place before greeting guests. Here, an overhead ceiling light, picture light attached to the mirror frame top, or a circular mirror with built-in lighting may be used. Lighting need not be overly critical for a last-minute check before opening the door.

Sunlamps

You can see them any weekend at the beach: oiled bodies lined up like sausage links on a great sandy skillet, all striving for that elusive "perfect tan." That healthy glow certainly makes people look better, and most claim they even feel better.

To answer the growing demand for an instant tan, franchised suntan salons are springing up around the country. Tanning salons, operating under names like Tan-trific, Plan-a-Tan, Tan Factory, and Sunburst International, offer their walk-in customers a daily dose of artificial sunshine. Depending on the lightness of a person's skin, treatments can range from 30 seconds to several minutes in a small booth equipped with 16 ultraviolet sunlamp bulbs. A typical customer commented, "I get white, pale, and peaked, and I don't like looking at myself. I feel a lot better about myself when I'm tan."

The tanning lights were first introduced in the late 1940s for dermatological use. The ultraviolet bulbs were developed by Westinghouse engineers with suggestions from skin specialists. Some dermatologists have been using the lamps for 30 years to treat acne and psoriasis patients.

While you can stop by your local tanning salon for a treatment, most people prefer to pamper themselves at home. It is less expensive, more convenient, and offers the privacy for 100 percent coverage. The ultimate in pleasure, stimulation, and comfort is the single-unit Habitat introduced by the Kohler Co., a bath fixture manufacturer. Their "environmental enclosure" is a small room

Photography: Bill Rooney

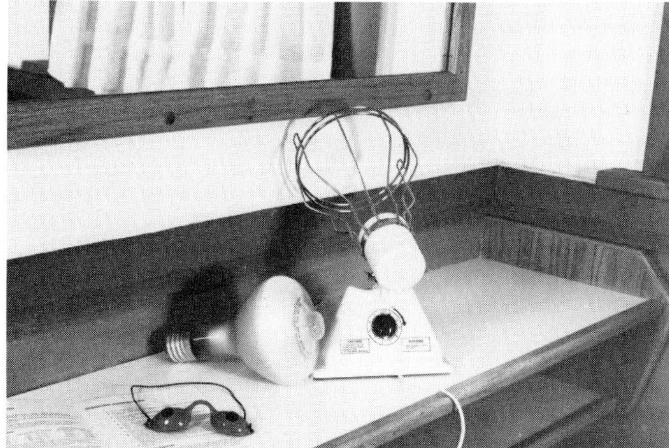

The sunlamp shown being installed in the photos above left is part of a kit that comes with the recommended timer and eye shields. These precautions are necessary to prevent healthful benefits from becoming harmful.

With Kohler's Habitat, above right, the user has the options of sunbathing in the Sun, rejuvenating in the Steam (an optional feature), or relaxing in the Rain. This new dimension in gracious living offers a total synthesis of man's natural environment.

equipped with four jet spray shower nozzles, steam bath controls that allow the steam to rise from beneath the redwood deck, a heater/blower combination to dry you with a warm breeze, and four overhead ultraviolet lamps to provide tanning sunlight.

An optional stereo package turns the Habitat into a bath entertainment center. It's an investment in self-indulgence costing as much as a new automobile. Depending on the size unit and options selected, you are looking at a $5,000 to $8,000 package. But if you are primarily interested in the benefits of a year-round tan, there are less expensive home systems.

Residential sunlamps range from $30 to less than $150, depending on the type and size unit. Less expensive models in the popular 275-watt lamp size are tabletop or wall-mounted, perhaps over a bath or dressing room mirror so that you can shave and tan at the same time each morning. Larger 400-watt models have a reflector area and may use bulb or quartz ultraviolet tanning tubes. Freestanding floor models of 800-watt capacity usually have detachable legs so the unit may be used on a tabletop. All but the least expensive models come equipped with built-in timers and include protective eye shields in the package.

RS sunlamp bulbs require a warmup period of about two minutes to reach full ultraviolet output, and, when shut off, the lamp must cool for approximately six minutes before it will restart. Sunlamp bulbs or tubes are rated by hours of performance. Higher rated lamps are more expensive initially, but less costly in the long term.

All approved sunlamps must be designed in accordance with the requirements of the American Medical Association as to the spectral distribution and erythemal effectiveness. Absorption of erythemal ultraviolet energy not only tans the skin, but also stimulates the formation of Vitamin D, which is the only vitamin that can be produced by the human body. The energy is known to play an important role in the deposition of calcium and may prevent rickets and be an effective aid in promoting soundness of bones and teeth.

Before using a sunlamp, you should check with your physician if you have highly sensitive skin, when using drugs or medication, or if you

Recommended Exposure Times

Bulb type sunlamps tend to be more concentrated in their tanning coverage.

Distance from Lamp	Diameter of Area Covered	Duration of Exposure: Sensitive skin	Average skin
30″	25″	4 min.	6 min.
36″	30″	6 min.	9 min.
48″	40″	10 min.	15 min.
60″	60″	16 min.	24 min.

Fluorescent sunlamps, available in 24- and 48-inch tube lengths, provide a wider tanning area coverage.

Type of Lamp	Distance From Lamp: One foot	Two feet	Three feet
20 watt + reflector	3 min.	7 min.	14 min.
20 watt bare bulb	8 min.	20 min.	41 min.
40 watt + reflector	2 min.	4 min.	6 min.
40 watt bare bulb	5 min.	10 min.	18 min.

have skin eruptions. In no case should exposure be repeated more frequently than once in a 24-hour period. Sunlamp treatments are not recommended for infants, and young children should receive one half the normal adult exposure time. See chart above for recommended exposure times.

For all their healthful benefits, sunlamps should be used with a certain amount of caution. Because the ultraviolet ray density close to the lamp is several times stronger than a midsummer sun, users should always protect their eyes and strictly follow manufacturer's recommended exposure times and distances to avoid serious burns. Sunglasses may be used, but most sunlamp kits include eye shields and timers. Be sure to use them as directed.

Sunglasses

Your eyes deserve protection from natural sunlight as well. Today there are styles, colors, and types of sunglasses to meet the needs of various outdoor activities. The early sunglasses were a simple green tint to reduce the impact of direct sunlight on the eye. To the original glass lenses were added the newer plastic lenses with lighter weight and shatterproof properties advisable for use during active sports.

The next major improvement was the introduction of Polaroid glasses. The elements within the glass itself were polarized or aligned much like a miniature venetian blind. Instead of just dampening the impact of direct sunlight as did the previous sunglasses, the Polaroid lens drastically reduced glare, yet retained a high degree of the original clarity.

The latest development is the light-sensitive or photochromic sunglasses. These self-adjusting lenses appear as clear glass when worn indoors. The lenses will darken in sunlight when exposed to natural ultraviolet rays, and the spectacles can act as sunglasses. When the wearer goes indoors or the sun clouds over, the glass returns to its clear state. On exposure to sunlight, light transmission decreases from 70 percent to 20 percent, and the process may take a gradual 15 to 20 minutes for complete color change.

One manufacturer of glasses for outdoor sportsmen suggests specific colors for individual activities: red-tinted glasses for trap, skeet, and pistol shooters on a bright, sunny

NuTone's surface-mounted Heat-A-Lite, above left, has a 1250-watt heater with one aluminum fan blade to force heat evenly throughout the room. White Lexan lenses at both ends of the fixture disperse bright light. Lens covers snap off for cleaning and bulb replacement.

Sears' 400-watt reflector sun and heat lamp has a 110-square-inch reflector area. It also includes a quartz ultraviolet tanning tube, two infrared heating rods, a 10-minute timer, a beige plastic case, an adjustable tilt base, and a pair of eye shields.

day; smoke or gray-tone for boaters and airplane pilots; brown-tone lenses for tennis, baseball, and other ground sports; on cloudy days, a yellow lens for rifle shooters.

Special sunglass designs are produced for the demands of different outdoor activities. For skiing, snowmobiling, and other cold weather sports, wraparound goggles are recommended. They provide wide-angle distortion-free viewing. Special plastic compound frames remain strong, flexible, and frost-free in extreme cold conditions. Most have an elastic adjustable head strap to fit around a helmet, and the goggles can be worn over eyeglasses. Shooters' glasses are hardened—treated for scratch resistance—and have semirimless frames to eliminate distortion and glare while sighting down a gun barrel. They are designed to ride high on the browline, have an adjustable nosepiece, and weigh about half as much as conventional sunglasses. Boaters' glasses are engineered to protect against the overhead sunlight and the harsh glare reflected off the water. One manufacturer even produces floating sunglasses with hollow frames for careless yachtsmen.

Heat Lamps

All incandescent light bulbs produce a certain amount of invisible infrared radiation as well as visible light. Infrared heat lamps are used for a number of baking, drying, and heating commercial applications, but two special lamp types are available for home use. Both are 250 watts in an R40 reflectorized bulb. One has clear glass, and the second is equipped with a red filter on the end that reduces the amount of visible light while continuing to transmit the infrared rays.

Heat is transferred by conduction, convection, or radiation. In conduction, the object is placed in physical contact with the heat source — an egg in a frying pan. In convection, the heat-source warm air heats the object — holding your hand over a lighted candle or the way a home is heated by a warm-air furnace. In radiation heating, however, the heat is transferred through invisible electromagnetic waves from an infrared source such as a heat lamp. When the infrared energy strikes an object, the radiation is absorbed and converted into heat. Radiant energy does not heat the air appreciably and does not require air

Photography: Karl Riek

This remodeled bathroom combines two important lighting elements: infrared heat lamps installed in the ceiling and incandescent globes surrounding the mirror. The glass-paned Dutch door, in place of a small window, provides another light source and gives access to the deck.

for transmission. Radiation is the way the earth, for instance, is heated by the sun.

Infrared heat lamps are most often installed in bathroom ceilings to provide some instant spot heating on a cold morning. Portable units are used in the bath or dressing area to dry hair or nail polish. Some of the better quality floor and tabletop model sunlamps also have heat lamps built into the same fixture. This setup allows you the option of tanning or heating or doing both simultaneously.

On the exterior, infrared heat lamps may be mounted on the wall or built into the overhead soffit to warm a deck or patio party during early spring or late fall evening entertaining.

As a health aid, the penetrating heat sensation from infrared energy is soothing to muscle aches and pains. Both the skin surface and the muscle layers beneath receive the soothing warmth from the lamp. Of course, infrared heat lamps, being at the opposite end of the visible spectrum from ultraviolet sunlamps, do not provide any tanning action, that is to say, heat lamps do not contain ultraviolet rays for tanning.

Safety Warning

You should be aware of a potential danger when using heat-producing appliances such as sun and heat lamps. Never use more than one heat-producing fixture on a standard 15-amp house current circuit at one time. The excessive energy demand will probably overload the circuit and blow a fuse or trip a circuit breaker.

Extension cords are not recommended for heavy current-pulling heat appliances. But if a cord is absolutely necessary, use one as short as possible—6 feet or less. And for safety, no extension cord should be smaller than #16-gauge wire.

Germicidal Lamps

Microbiology is the world of unseen life, the world of bacteria, mold spores, yeast, and virus. Each of these is a microbe, a tiny living cell. The air may contain countless bacteria and mold spores that are the cause of spoilage in perishable foods and the source of disease in persons and animals.

Sunlight, which includes ultraviolet energy, is effective in killing many

Miami-Carey's new ventilator/light combination, above right, is beautiful and practical. The unit can be wired so that fan and light turn on simultaneously or separately. A white molded grille and pebblegrained light diffuser are an effective touch to any room's decor.

NuTone's fixture, above left, combines heating, ventilation, and light in one installation. All may operate together, individually, or in any combination. The unit includes an on/off switch with ivory knobs mounted on a gold-finish plate. The heating element is 1500 watts with automatic thermal protection.

forms of bacteria. But indoors the air is relatively confined and often contaminated with germs. Germicidal lamps are effective in wiping out a variety of harmful bacteria. The lamps are a source of ultraviolet radiation having a wave length of 2537 angstroms, fatal to many types of bacteria and mold.

Industry has used germicidal lamps in restaurants, beauty parlors, barber shops, hospitals, and rest rooms. Food processers, meat packers, dairy and poultry farms, and veterinarians employ germicidal lamps to maintain or create sanitary conditions.

In the home, germicidal lamps can be installed in the heating or air conditioning duct work to purify the air as it circulates throughout the house. Other installations go right to the heart of the problem. The lamps have been used in the kitchen and bath areas to eliminate bacteria and mold. Laundries and other high-moisture spots within the house are controlled with the microbe-killing ultraviolet radiation. Pet areas, kennels, and barns use the germicidal lamps to destroy airborne microorganisms and maintain sanitary environments.

Germicidal fixtures should be installed carefully so that people and pets receive no direct radiation. Safe practices call for installing indirect fixtures or fixtures with directional louvers on the wall or suspended from the ceiling above eye level. In this way the upper air in the room is completely irradiated with the ultraviolet rays, but none of the rays reach the occupants of the room. This method of air disinfection is quite efficient because the normal air currents and drafts in the room cause the bacteria in the air to rise and fall from floor to ceiling many times an hour.

Germicidal lamps are available in a number of wattages and sizes. The 8-, 15- and 30-watt sizes are designed to operate with standard fluorescent fixtures. U-shaped tubes and screw-in bulbs are also available on the market.

Ozone Lamps

"They just don't build houses like they used to." In most cases, today's house is considerably better constructed than its predecessor. The earlier houses may have been structurally sound, but they were much draftier than the modern ones.

Detjen's heavy-duty insect electrocutor, above left, intercepts and counter-attracts night insects with a filtered black light and destroys them electrically. No more will seasonal insect infestation ruin your outdoor gatherings.

Above right, Charmglow's electric bug killer attracts unwanted pests with a 30-watt black light and a blue bulb. The unit destroys bugs cleanly and efficiently. Most bug killers are available in interior and exterior models. Be sure to specify location when you purchase a unit.

In our concern for energy conservation with additional wall and roof insulation, complete window and door weatherstripping, and double and triple window glazing, we have created living spaces that no longer have the chance to "breathe."

These efficient, airtight, draft-free houses have created serious odor problems through lack of air circulation. It's a combination of household cleaning chemicals, cooking, people, and pet odors. And the smell of a "ripe" cigar may last for days. Even more serious is the growing concern over harmful formaldehyde emission odors from building materials, carpets, drapes, and clothing found in the home.

The ozone lamp is a close cousin to the ultraviolet germicidal lamp. It develops ozone, a form of oxygen, which destroys odor. The best description of ozone is that feeling in the air after a thunder storm has passed through.

Unlike room fresheners, which attempt to mask odors with a perfumed scent, the ozone lamp goes to the heart of the problem and eliminates the offending odor. You may have a difficult time locating ozone lamps through normal lighting supply sources, but they are available through commercial supply houses.

Bug Lights

The term "bugs" covers all those pesky light-sensitive flying insects such as mosquitoes, moths, gnats, and midges, as well as the common housefly. While some insects are just plain bothersome, others, like the mosquito and housefly, are classified as more dangerous pestilence-carrying insects. Recent research indicates that there are more than 87,000 different fly species, and a single fly can carry more than 33 million disease-causing micro-organisms.

Lights available to fight the flying insect battle include three distinct types and methods: light that illuminates without attracting the insect; light that repels the insects; and light fixtures that destroy them.

The simplest antibug light has been around for a number of years. It is a yellow, regular-shaped incandescent bulb often seen on porches or garages. Night-flying insects are attracted by the blue light spectrum found in ordinary bulbs. The special yellow coating in bug lights filters out the blue. Insects can-

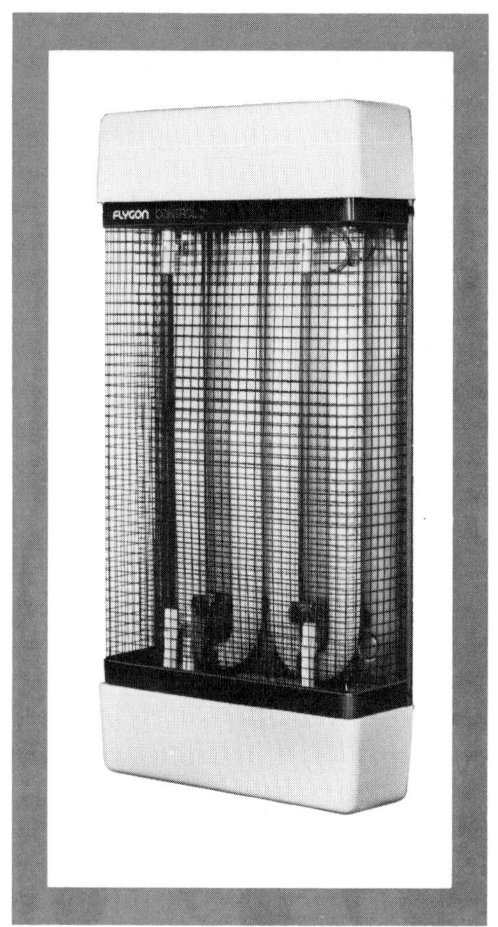

Flowtron manufactures Electronic Insect Control Units like this Fly Control Model FC-8500, shown above left. The unit combines 90 watts of black light energy with an exclusive "glo-tube" to make a powerfully effective insect killer that is ecologically safe and economical to operate.

The Flygon Control 2 electric bug killer shown above right is made by Charmglow. The grille is sized to allow small pests to penetrate, but is designed to exclude butterflies, bees, birds, and other helpful insects.

not see this light as well and are less likely to be attracted to it.

Insects, of course, can see regular bulbs at night. Therefore, if you leave regular interior lights shining through the window, a yellow bulb on the porch will have little effect. The yellow bulb does not attract insects, but also it does not repel them. Bug lights are available in 60-, 100- and 150-watt sizes.

A small, pleasant light that will repel bugs during evening and also during daylight hours is a citronella candle. Citronella, with a lemon-like odor, is derived from a fragrant grass grown in southern Asia. It is cultivated as a source of oil used in liniment, perfume soap, and as an insect repellant when added to candles. When burned in attractive glass holders, the votive-size citronella candles can do an effective job in eliminating bothersome insects from patios, decks, and gardens.

With the growing objection to the use of chemical insecticides and sprays, electric bug killers have gained in popular use. Unlike chemicals, the electrocutors are completely safe for humans and pets.

The fixtures use a special black light or black light-blue lamp to attract mosquitoes, gnats, moths, flies, and other pests to an electrically charged grid and kills them instantly. The unit has a protective grill to keep birds or fingers from accidentally touching the power source. The grille is sized to allow the small pests to penetrate, but is designed to exclude butterflies, bees, and other helpful insects.

Most electronic bug killers use a black light-blue fluorescent tube for general conditions, and a few have blue incandescent bulbs. Where flies are a particular problem, a black light or black light combined with a black light-blue is recommended. Flies generally require more visible light from the black light to attract them.

Unlike the yellow bulbs and citronella candles, the electronic bug killers draw the insects toward the fixture. Because of this attraction, it is suggested that the fixtures be mounted on poles, to buildings, or hung from trees away from the activity area. Place them 25 to 50 feet from patios, gardens, and decks, and the ideal location is between your home and a natural insect source, such as a nearby swamp or pond. The units are most effective 8 to 10 feet from ground level.

Special attention should be given to the quality and quantity of exterior lights for safety and security. Fixtures should complement the architectural details of the home. Shown here is the New Orleans Heritage Series from Lightcraft of California.

9 Light for Safety

Annually, the National Safety Council compiles a set of frightening statistics cataloging accidents and deaths suffered by the American public. Through better automotive design, reduced highway speeds, and improved traffic control systems, accidents per passenger mile are being reduced. Industry has done a highly credible job working with unions, the Occupational Safety & Health Administration, and insurance companies to improve manufacturing conditions. Unfortunately, too many accidents, and even deaths, still occur in the home.

Safe home lighting is a combination of common sense, convenience, and careful planning. With today's technology and coordinated groups of fixtures matched in styling to the architectural character of your home, safe lighting can add to the comfort and personality of your house for a minimum investment.

Safe Exterior Lighting

Your front entry area should be the focal point of your outdoor lighting efforts. Here, you can establish a warm, friendly welcome to your home, and provide safe lighting for family and guests.

Where possible, a pair of wall-bracket fixtures should be installed on both sides of the entryway. Fixtures should be located approximately 66 inches above the porch surface. Fixtures with an 8-inch or larger diameter are ideal, with a 6-inch diameter the suggested minimum. Normally, 60-watt bulbs are used in each bracket, but where the brackets are spaced far apart, 75- or 100-watt bulbs will supply the necessary lighting.

If space permits only a single wall-mounted fixture, install it at the same height on the lock or handle side of the door. Where your architecture does not lend itself to wall fixtures, consider locating a single large fixture directly over the doorway, or mounting a recessed light in the porch ceiling or roof overhang. Try to position the fixture so that sufficient illumination is cast on the doorway, porch surface, and any adjacent steps. Suggested minimum for these fixtures is 100 watts.

Several additional lighting ideas for a safe and convenient entry include lighted house numbers, illuminated door bell buttons, and lighted locks, which eliminate awkward fumbling with keys. All are low-wattage fixtures requiring little energy demand.

Other home entry points, back and side doors, should receive the same careful lighting approach. However, these less public locations can usually be successfully illuminated with a single 100-watt fixture. A convenient wall switch inside the door allows lights to be controlled as you enter or leave.

Additional safety lighting, which can be attached to the house, includes recessed fixtures in the soffit along the front of the house to act as exterior wall washers, and spotlights recessed into the roof overhang to accent architectural lines or light up walkway and entrances. Similar ideas can work effectively to light up large porches, breezeways, and patio areas.

Like your entryway, garage doors can be lit by a pair of flanking wall-

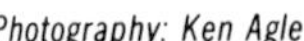

Photography: Ken Agle

Heritage Lanterns has created these wall-mounted bracket fixtures, above left. Installation of these fixtures on either side of the entry door is the safest plan. Normally, 60-watt bulbs are used in each bracket, but where the brackets are spaced far apart, 75- or 100-watt bulbs are preferred.

Outdoor living areas like the deck above right require floodlights for nighttime use. Properly lit, decks and patios can be transformed into extensions of the relaxation and/or entertaining areas of the interior of your home. A well-lighted deck can also discourage intruders.

mounted fixtures or directional spotlights installed near the roof peak. A single-car garage interior should have two lamps or fixtures mounted on either side about six feet from the front bumper, to light passageways at the sides of the car. A two-car or larger garage will require a minimum of three lights, to cover the sides and center area effectively.

For general yard lighting to provide wide area coverage, mount a single or double weatherproof, adjustable floodlight unit at second-story level, under eaves or roof overhang. Tall trees or freestanding poles also may be used. PAR-38 floodlight bulbs of 75 or 150 watts are usually recommended, but you may want to consider the more efficient mercury, sodium, or other high-intensity discharge lamps. While they produce more light with less energy, and they last considerably longer, these lamps do not deliver a "white" light. The green, yellow, or purple cast, seen in stadium or supermarket parking lots, is not always considered attractive to homeowners.

Drives, walkways, and steps deserve special attention when planning safe exterior lighting. A post lantern, a minimum of 12 inches square or diameter, set 66 inches above ground level, can be used to locate a main entrance walkway or driveway. Most use a 75-watt bulb, but the newer 50-watt white mercury lamps supply as much light as a 100-watt conventional bulb. When planning your safety lighting for steps and longer stairways, use enough fixtures to provide uniform illumination. Both the horizontal treads and the vertical risers should be fully lit.

Low level mushroom lamps or small spotlights are usually strung along driveways and walkways for attractive and safe lighting. Individual units, or a kit with strings of fixtures prewired, are available with white or colored lights.

When selecting outdoor fixtures, avoid those with clear glass and brightly exposed high-wattage bulbs. For safe lighting, you need illumination without glare. Frosted or tinted glass, fixtures designed to throw light downward, and careful placement of the fixtures will prevent after-image glare, which hampers seeing and can itself cause accidents.

Typical exterior wiring requires that all connections be watertight and wiring be protected from physical damage. Three-wire cable is required to

Illustration source: Westinghouse Electric

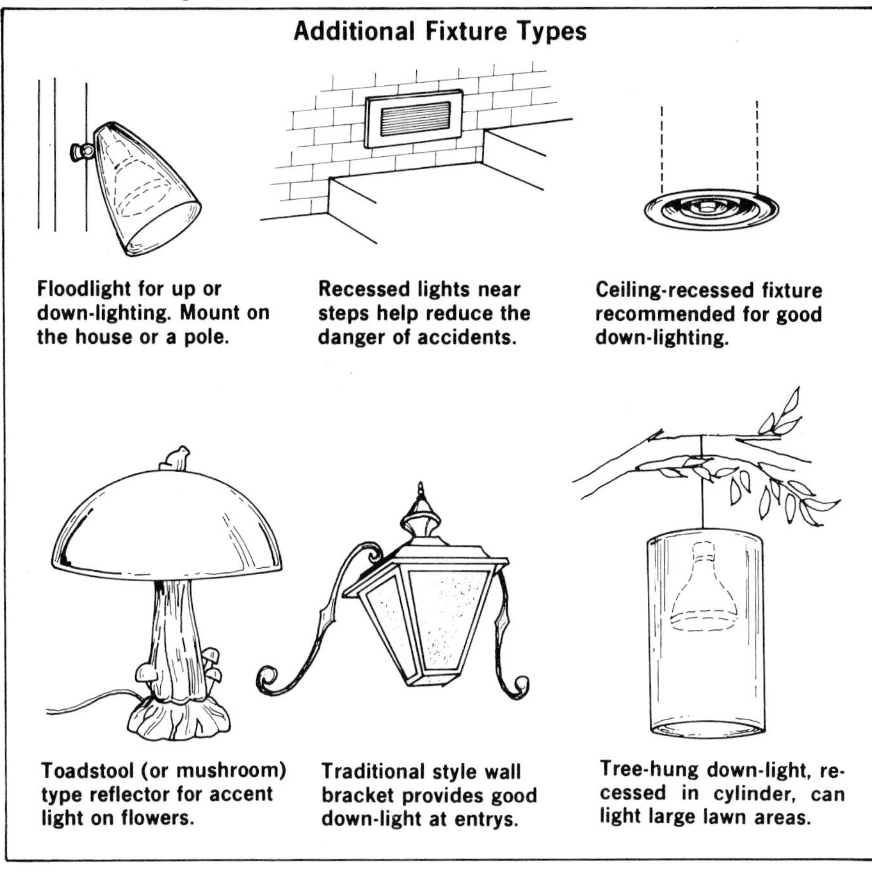

This freestanding post lantern fixture from Heritage Lanterns, above, shows how exterior lighting fixtures can become a part of your landscaping. Rather than leaving the post starkly exposed, you can train a vine around it and plant flowers or low shrubbery around base.

provide ground protection, and ground-fault interrupters must be used for outdoor receptacle circuits and underwater pool lighting circuits. A standard 120-volt outdoor system falls under regulation of your local municipal electrical codes, and all work requires inspection for approval. In most cases, exterior lighting is not a job for the amateur. You'll need professional help.

However, the modern low-voltage outdoor lighting systems, which operate on 12-volt rather than the 120-volt house power, offer some real advantages to the homeowner. The low-voltage systems are available in kit form, are easier to install, more convenient to use, and can save you up to 80 percent compared to conventional systems.

The kits consist of a transformer to step down the power to a safer 12-volt range. This greatly reduces the hazard of outdoor lighting to pets, children, and careless use of power mowers. Usually six or eight mushroom lamps or small spotlights, plus connectors and underground cable, are included. The system is prewired to snap or plug together for quickest possible assembly.

Once installed, some systems may be unplugged. When the light post is removed, the receptacle remains flush in the ground, and you can run the lawnmower safely over the top. The low-voltage systems are ideal for lighting along a walkway, drive, or surrounding a pool.

They provide an additional energy-saving bonus. Each of the 12-volt lamps, in a typical system, run on only 18 watts of power, so six 12-volt lamps require the same energy as a single 120-volt spotlight.

A photo-electric eye, installed in your entryway lighting or post lantern, will automatically activate these fixtures as dusk approaches. There is nothing more inviting than a warm and safely lit home to welcome family and friends.

Safe Interior Lighting

All interior home lighting must conform to electrical code requirements. However, you should understand that building and electrical code specifications represent the legal minimum, and not necessarily the most ideal lighting system. In all cases, you must meet minimum code requirements, but you should consider additional fixtures for both convenience and safety.

Courtesy of Woodbridge Ornamental Iron Co.

A spiral staircase like the one at right needs good lighting all along its descent. The hanging fixtures illuminate the top half of the stairs, while the large spots on the bottom level provide visibility for the rest of the way.

An entry door should have a light switch immediately inside, so that the room may be illuminated without the hazard of walking into a dark area to fumble for a table lamp. The same rule holds true for all rooms in the house—a handy light switch immediately inside each door.

Hallways and stairs are common places where falls and serious accidents occur. In these potentially dangerous locations, lighting controls, as well as adequate illumination, are important for safety. Three-way switches should be installed at the foot and top of stairs, and at each end of long hallways. This system allows lights to be turned on at one location and switched off after passing through a hall or stairway.

Curved or angled stairways may need a light positioned in the center, as well as at the top and bottom, to provide adequate illumination for treads and risers. Wall- or ceiling-mounted fixtures, with a minimum 60-watt bulb, are usually adequate. Long, narrow halls should have fixtures spaced every eight to ten feet. Those with higher than average ceilings (in older homes) require wallmounted or drop fixtures, rather than ceiling recessed models. As with your exterior lighting, position fixtures to eliminate any dangerous glare. Shielding against top viewing of bulbs is particularly essential where stairways descend into a hall area.

For some reason, unfinished basements, attics, or large walk-in closets never seem to have adequate lighting. Too often, these dim areas are the scene of avoidable home accidents. If wiring for conventional fixtures is difficult, consider using self-contained wireless, or battery-operated, lights to overcome the problem. The small, inexpensive units can be easily mounted and, since they operate on standard "D" flashlight size batteries, need no external wiring. Most are activated by a switch or pull chain, but some models are self-activating and light when a closet or attic door is opened.

Bathrooms present a special safety hazard because of excessive moisture conditions. No fixtures, switches, or outlets should be located close to a tub or shower where a person could possibly touch the electrical circuits while standing in water. Safety experts are concerned about the increased use of electrical appliances in the bath area—everything from electric razors and

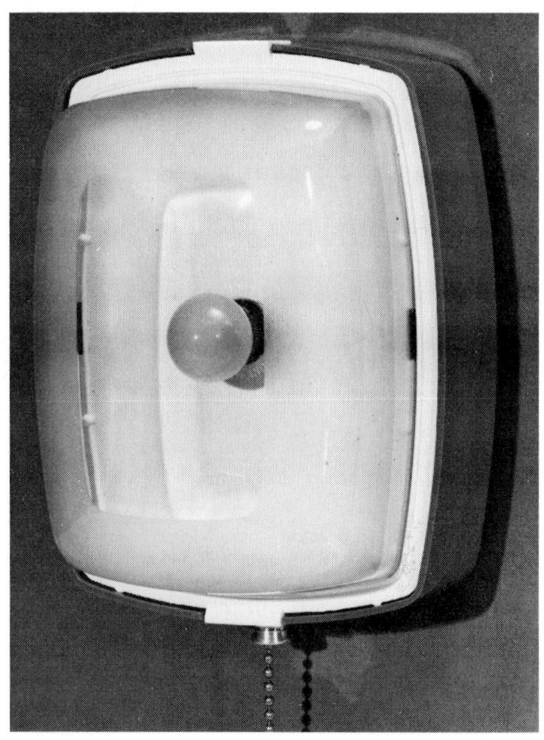

Sears' Sensor Lite, above left, is a photoelectrical cell that can be used in any home electrical outlet. A light-sensitive eye adjusts bulb intensity throughout the day and into the night without the aid of switches or timers. The solid-state component can be used in any room in the house.

Sears offers a self-contained wireless, battery-operated area light, above right. Fixtures like these are ideal for hard-to-light places like unfinished basements, attics, or large walk-in closets. Wiring for conventional fixtures may be difficult in these areas, hence the need for self-contained units.

hair dryers to sun lamps and toothbrushes. To minimize the risk of receiving an electrical shock while standing on a damp bath mat, all appliances and outlets should have three-wire circuits and three-prong plugs for safe grounding.

Young children have a natural fear of the darkness, which can lead to unfortunate accidents. A small night-light in the bedroom and bath can help correct this potential danger. The most popular night-light is a 7-watt bulb rated at 3,000 hours. A 15-watt, switched wall bracket, or 4-watt plug-in type, are also available. The smallest "darkness chaser" for children is a tiny neon light rated at 1/4-watt—a real energy miser.

Home Fire Protection

The figures are frightening. More than 750,000 homes are damaged by fire each year resulting in some 7,000 deaths annually. Although the United States is technically the most advanced nation in the world, we suffer the highest rate of death-per-million population due to fire.

Too often we think that statistics of this nature only apply to other families. Yet, the National Commission on Fire Prevention and Control warns that chances are that the average family will experience a serious home fire at least every generation.

Prior to 1974, residential fire protection systems were mostly limited to apartment complexes, but rapid expansion is occurring because of the increasing number of multifamily dwellings, greater power usage in single-family homes, and stiffer municipal fire codes. Two-thirds of the states have regulations requiring the use of smoke alarms, usually in new housing development projects and mobile homes. Some states, like Oregon, have expanded legislation to require smoke detectors in all existing rental living units—houses, apartments, lodging houses, motels and hotels—and owner-occupied, single-family residences when they change owners. When an existing home is sold, a certificate of smoke detector installation must be filed with the Fire Marshall's office.

Most fire-related accidents and deaths might well be prevented if an early warning is given at the beginning of a fire. Unfortunately, statistics disclose that the majority of destructive and fatal fires occur between 9 p.m. and 6 a.m. when

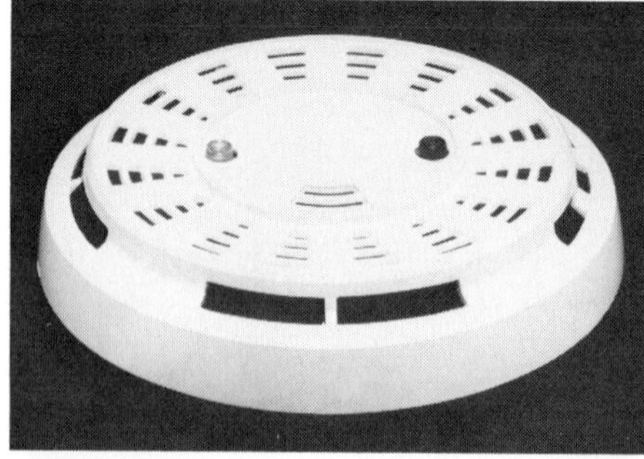

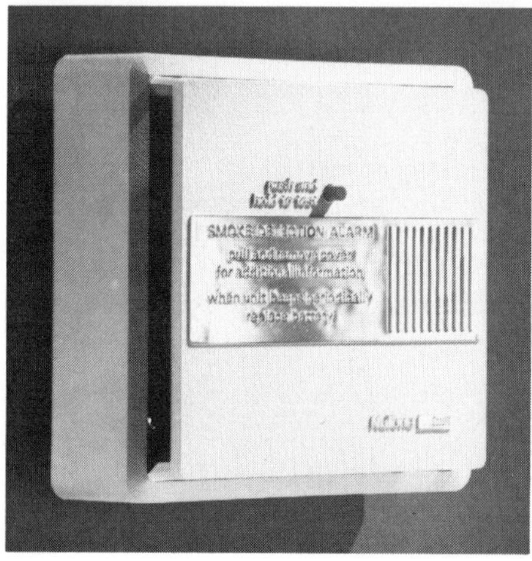

Where to locate your smoke detection alarm

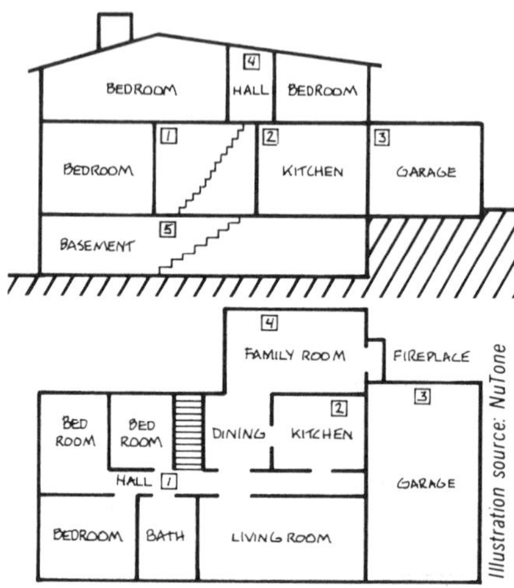

Install at least one on each floor in multilevel homes.

This smoke detector from Sears, above, features a built-in transmitter that sends signals from remote areas of the house to a special receiver that sounds an emergency warning. A test button to make sure the unit is still operating is a valuable addition.

Sears' photo-ionization smoke detector, upper right, combines the principles of photoelectric and ionization sensors to make these detectors more sensitive to fires.

NuTone's new battery-operated smoke detector, lower right, operates on the photoelectric principle. It is open on four sides to permit smoke to enter the chamber from any direction. Its 9-volt alkaline battery has an approximate life of one year. A trouble alarm of beeping signals when the battery needs replacing.

victims are asleep, and the senses are dulled. The first three to five minutes of a fire are the most critical if victims are to escape the effects of smoke and fire gases—the killing elements in four out of five fatalities.

There are two types of fire detectors on the market today: heat detectors and smoke detectors. The heat detectors are either a *fixed temperature* device, usually set to sound an alarm when air temperature reaches 135 degrees Fahrenheit, or *rate-of-rise* detectors that have no fixed temperature figure, but are activated when temperatures rise faster than expected under normal household conditions. Heat detectors react too slowly to be used as early warning devices and are not approved for sleeping or living areas.

Only the smoke detector can give an early enough warning of smoke and lethal gases to allow a family to escape safely. *Photo-electric* smoke detectors are activated when rising smoke and gas interrupt a small light beam in the unit, reflecting the light onto a light-sensitive photocell that triggers the alarm. *Ionization detectors* are sensitive to microscopic, airborne, combustion particles, which impede the flow of electric current in the unit setting off the alarm.

Buying and Using Alarms

A safe home fire alarm system must conform to the following:

1. Produce an alarm loud enough and long enough to awaken a family. At least 85 decibels of noise lasting several minutes is the accepted minimum.

2. Be a quality unit, simple to install, maintain, and be free from possible false alarm malfunctions.

3. Be self-supervising to signify weak batteries, mechanical breakdown, or other problems canceling operating efficiency.

Before buying a home alarm system, you should contact your local fire department to request their help in selecting the right type, number, and placement of alarms for your home. Most recommend that several smoke alarms be placed between the sleeping areas and the rest of the house. In low ceiling homes, they may be mounted on the ceiling. Older homes with high ceilings usually have the units installed a foot or more down the wall. Plug-in units operate off the normal house current, or battery models are available.

Smoke alarms are your first line of

Fire Alarm Safety

1. Install smoke alarms to protect all sleeping areas.
2. Use heat detectors to back up your system in heating and cooking areas.
3. All alarms should conform to standards set by Factory Mutual or Underwriters' Laboratories.
4. Check alarms for operating efficiency on a regular schedule.
5. Develop and rehearse a safe family evacuation plan.

Pittway's First Alert smoke detector, above, features the double protection of a combination photoelectric and ionization unit. The new smoke detector is powered by 9-volt batteries and sounds an 85-decibel horn for the alarm.

safety but, if possible, several heat detector alarms should be installed in the basement, kitchen, or other areas where flaming rather than smoking fires may occur.

While your local fire department will be quite helpful, they cannot supply brand or manufacturers' names. For a listing of approved fire alarm devices, write to the Underwriters' Laboratories and ask for a copy of their "Fire Protection Equipment" list. Check with your insurance company for possible discounts on your homeowner's policy.

Once your alarms are installed, read the manufacturer's directions carefully and set up a regular periodic testing schedule using a cigarette or burning match. Malfunctioning or dead battery alarms are worse than useless because they give a false sense of security.

Residential smoke detectors are important but represent only the first step in a safe escape plan. The stress situation presented by a fire or inhaling low levels of carbon monoxide can cause panic. Establish an emergency plan ahead of time, so that all members of your family know what to do if the alarm sounds in the middle of the night. Speed is vital. Don't attempt to fight the fire. Evacuate all family members immediately, and call the fire department from a neighbor's house. Once outside, never reenter the home. Your concern is the safety of your family. Let the insurance company worry about the house and its contents.

Extension Cords

Handy extension cords are so familiar that we too often forget that they can represent a real danger if not used properly. Overload them and you may blow a fuse or burn out an appliance. Damaged cords can result in severe burns, a fatal shock, or a tragic fire.

The ordinary household extension cord is usually constructed of No. 18, two-wire lamp cord with a protective plastic coating. The most popular lengths are 6 and 9 feet, but these two-prong, low-power cords are available in 3- to 20-foot lengths.

Heavier-duty yellow or orange extension cords are flat and contain a third grounding wire and double-weight insulation. They are UL-listed for indoor use only. Where extension cords are subjected to heavy use and constant flexing, such as with portable power tools, the

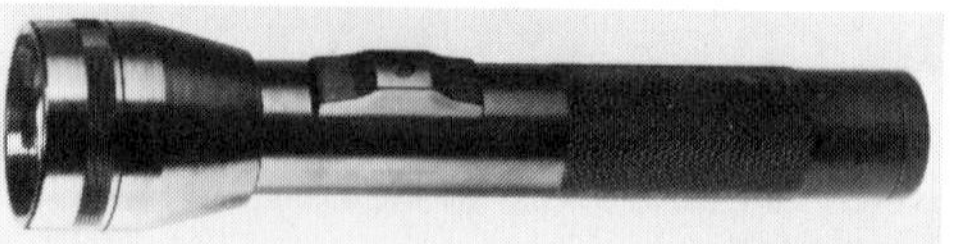

Extension Cord Wire Gauge Size
Extension cord length

Amps	25 ft.	50 ft.	75 ft.	100 ft.
2	18	18	18	16
4	18	18	16	14
6	18	16	14	14
8	18	16	14	12
10	16	14	12	12
12	14	14	12	12
14	14	12	10	10
16	12	12	10	10
18	12	12	10	8
20	12	10	8	8

Brookstone's emergency light, above left, automatically goes on when the power goes off. Just plug the powerful little light into any 115-volt AC wall socket. The light stays on for about 50 minutes once the power drops below 45 volts. It automatically shuts off and begins recharging when power is restored.

The emergency light by Archer, shown above right, also automatically goes on when the power goes off. It, too, plugs into any standard wall socket. The small, handsized unit can double as a flashlight.

Brookstone's heavy-duty flashlight, above right, is made of durable aircraft aluminum, ¼ inch thick. It is made to withstand abuse from dropping, bumping, or dunking. The shockproof bulb mounting preserves the lens and bulb from hard knocks. A precision-shaped reflector assures a strong beam.

heavy-duty, round, three-wire cords are recommended.

To be UL-listed for outdoor use for power mowers or hedge clippers, a three-wire round cord must have connector and cap molded to the cord insulation.

When buying a new extension cord, you need to consider three points: the cord length, the load capacity in amps, and the connectors. The load-carrying capacity of a cord is determined by the size of the wire and the length of the cord. The thinner the wire, the lower the capacity and the shorter the distance it will efficiently conduct electricity.

As a guideline for selecting the proper size and length extension cord, use the chart above.

Extension Cord Safety Tips

1. Buy only UL-approved cords and plugs that have been inspected for safety requirements.

2. Select the proper size and length cord to handle specific tasks and loads.

3. Don't overload cords. No more than one appliance operating at one time per cord.

4. Don't use a small lamp cord on a heating appliance. They are not designed for this use and will overheat and/or burn out the appliance.

5. Never run an extension cord under a rug or carpet, over radiators or pipes, or fasten in place with nails or staples through cord.

6. Inspect cords regularly for worn spots, cracked or brittle insulation, or exposed wiring, and replace.

Emergency Home Lighting

When the power fails and the house is suddenly cloaked in darkness, all lighting theory goes out the window. What you need now, and in a hurry, is emergency lighting. Several organizations, such as Brookstone and Radio Shack, offer the perfect solution to these "sudden darkness" situations—an emergency light that automatically goes on when the power goes off. The small, hand-size units plug into any standard 115-volt wall socket. As the power drops to 45 volts or less, or goes off completely, a bright light comes on automatically. The light can then be removed and used as a flashlight. Once the emergency is over, simply plug the light back into the wall socket and it recharges itself.

Selecting an Emergency Flashlight

1. Buy quality and rugged construction. In an emergency, performance is more important than price.
2. A wide beam rather than narrow beam is the best general use choice.
3. A 2 or 3 "D" battery size is the most convenient model to store and use.
4. Batteries should load from the rear rather than the top to avoid removing lens, reflector, and bulb.
5. A quick on-off or flash button switch is preferred.
6. A hook or clip on the barrel is handy, and consider a magnetic case for shop and auto. It also provides a nonrollable feature.
7. A plastic rather than glass lens is a safety benefit.
8. Select a light-colored plastic or shiny metal case for visibility in dark areas.

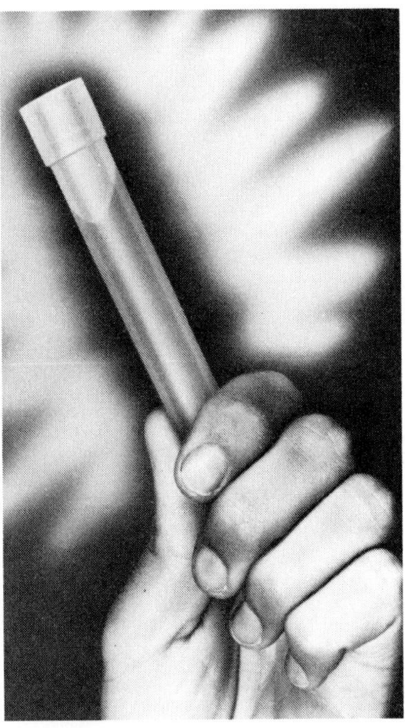

This plug-in handheld searchlight by Brookstone, above left, is designed for use in your car, truck, boat, or small plane. It will shine with no reflection through windshields, and down through fog, rain, haze, and mist.

Chemical photo luminescence is the principle operating this emergency handheld light by Brookstone, above right. It is activated only when you break the inner vial containing the chemical catalyst. The bright glow provides instant three-hour light, followed by a soft glow for 24 hours.

The automatic emergency light is just the item needed to provide instant light while you hunt up regular flashlights throughout the house. Every home should have several in good working order, with fresh batteries. Flashlights come in a bewildering array of sizes and designs. Some are standard two- and three-battery models, some range from penlight to lantern size, and both rechargeable and hand-squeeze chargeable styles are available. If you are tired of ordinary flashlights with corroded insides, dented or cracked bodies, and broken lenses, then perhaps you should invest in what Brookstone calls "The world's finest, toughest, most reliable flashlight with a lifetime guarantee." It's used by police, firemen, pilots, and others who need a dependable light. Rugged, shockproof, and waterproof, it is totally rust- and corrosion-resistant inside and out, all for \$20-\$25, batteries not included.

In a sudden emergency, most homes are better equipped than people realize. Your fireplace can supply light, heat, and serve as a rallying place for the family. Camping equipment, particularly propane, gasoline, or kerosene lanterns and stoves, can carry you through a crisis in relative comfort. Decorative candles or brass lanterns used on the dining room table can be placed throughout a darkened house. If you live in hurricane or tornado areas, special emergency candles are a good investment. The candle is formed by compressing paraffin under pressure, and although small in size, it burns for nearly three days.

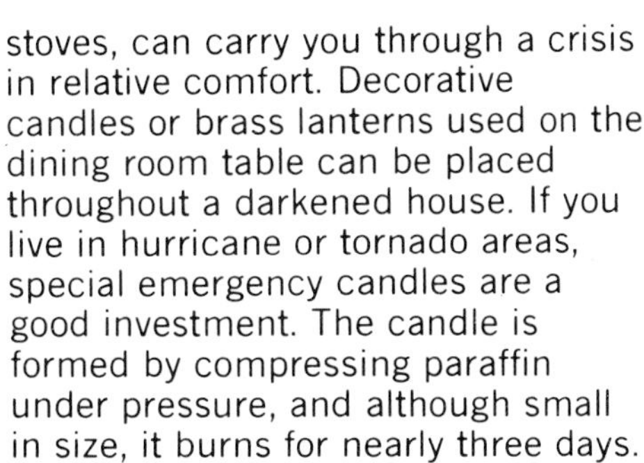

For automotive and boating emergencies, road flares or flare guns should be standard equipment. New lighting equipment that operates off a 12-volt DC cigarette lighter receptacle includes regular incandescent spotlights and floodlights, fluorescent tubes, and super-bright quartz-halogen spotlights.

The most revolutionary light today operates by chemical photo luminesence. It sounds like something from outer space, but it operates on the same principle used by fireflies. To activate the emergency light, simply bend a plastic tube slightly to break and release a chemical catalyst inside. The intense glow lasts over three hours and gradually fades for as long as 24 hours. It is a safe, ideal emergency light.

Photography: General Electric

This entryway demonstrates proper precautions taken against intruders. The shrubbery has been trimmed so the front entrance is visible to neighbors. Spotlights have been mounted in front of the door. The interior also gives the impression of people within.

10 Light for Security

While a man's home may be his castle, it takes more than a moat full of hungry crocodiles to make that home secure from intruders.

Of the three million burglaries reported each year, more than 60 percent are committed on residences. According to the FBI, burglaries are increasing at an 8 percent annual rate, and the total annual loss to homeowners exceeds $1 billion. Experts predict that one out of every five homes in the U.S. will be burglarized within the next 12-15 months.

Can a family make its home or apartment secure today? Professional criminals and law enforcement officials agree that a determined and experienced burglar cannot be stopped, short of installing Fort Knox-type anti-intruder systems. However, both groups do admit that a few simple measures, taken by the average homeowner, can discourage most amateur thieves and many professionals. If you can make the job look difficult enough, burglars will pass up your home in favor of an easier mark. You may not always be able to provide 100 percent security, but you certainly can improve the odds in your favor.

To make your home more secure, there are three basic steps you should follow:

1. Give the impression that you are home even when you are not. Burglars look for an unoccupied house to attack. The last thing they need is confrontation with an irate homeowner.

2. Make your home look hard to break into. Most amateur thieves will be discouraged, and even a professional will not want to risk the time and noise necessary to enter a secure house.

3. A well-organized security system draws too much attention. Perimeter alarms or entry alarms that activate clanging gongs, screaming sirens, and flashing lights usually force a burglar into a quick retreat before neighbors and police can arrive.

Don't Look Like a Victim

Some homes just beg to be robbed. Garage doors are left wide open, windows ajar, notes pinned to the front door telling friends when you will return. Newspapers and mail pile up while owners are away, the lawn goes unmowed, and door keys are hidden in the mailbox, under the flower pot, or under the doormat. These security crimes of negligence are usually committed by the very people who complain loudest about the soaring cost of homeowner and burglary insurance.

Pretend you are a thief and spend a few minutes casing your own home. Are doors and windows securely locked? Are many lights and radio or TV noise evident at night? Are ground-level windows and back doors screened from a neighbor's view by shrubs and tall hedges? Can you peer through your windows and spot expensive TV sets, stereos, tape decks, camera equipment, and other portable and valuable items?

Many home security measures are just plain common sense. Don't hide keys on your property; leave them with a neighbor. If you are away on vacation, arrange to have the lawn cut, have newspaper and mail

Illustration source: NuTone

The illustration above shows how inviting an unlighted house can be to a burglar. If you can peer through windows and spot valuables, remove them. Several lights in interior rooms provide a good deception, but better is a system of timed lights and appliances.

deliveries held for later collection, lock all house and garage doors and windows, and remove all tempting valuables from plain sight.

When you are away for a short time, leave lights on in several interior rooms, play a radio for noise, and leave drapes and shades slightly ajar to add to the house's lived-in appearance. If you don't have one, your smartest move may be to acquire a dog. Your home is more than ten times as likely to be invaded by a burglar if you don't have a small, yapping animal to set up a racket.

Exterior Lighting

Given the time and privacy needed to exercise his criminal talents, any thief can generally open a residential lock or outwit a home alarm system. Darkness provides the natural concealment for his crimes. Eliminate that concealment and you have raised the odds dramatically in your favor. Cut back shrubbery and trim down hedges along the sides and rear of your house so that the area is visible from the street or neighboring houses. Your entry lights can be supplemented by inexpensive floodlights that will eliminate those dark corners where a prowler might lurk. This coverage should include the sides and back of your house for maximum security.

Spotlights or floodlights can be mounted directly on the house siding, above or under the eaves, or installed on freestanding poles or tall trees within the yard. Consult the fixture manufacturer for information on the proper mounting height to gain maximum illumination from a particular type bulb and fixture. Incandescent bulbs can be used for exterior lighting, but PAR or high-intensity discharge lamps provide more light with less energy, and last considerably longer. High efficiency and long-term maintenance benefits are the prime reasons these newer lights have gained popularity for security use.

Low-wattage mercury lamps have replaced traditional incandescent fixtures in some cases, but the blue-green color may be unacceptable in some applications. Halide lamps combine the efficiency of fluorescent lamps with the color fidelity of incandescent lamps. They are 50 percent more efficient than mercury, and five times that of incandescent.

High-pressure sodium lamps have a distinctive golden cast to their light.

Illustration source: Westinghouse

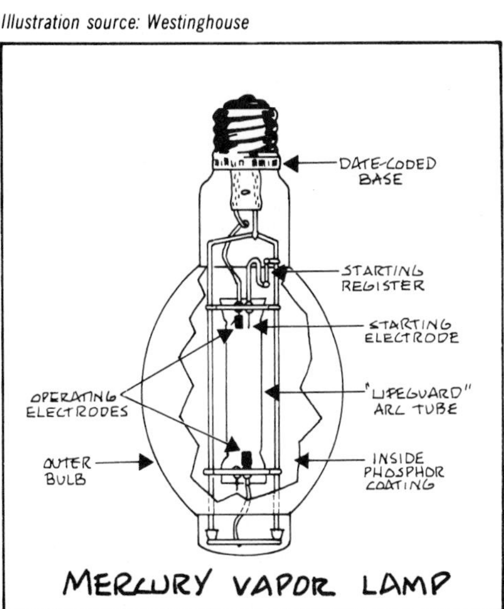

Illustration source: Westinghouse

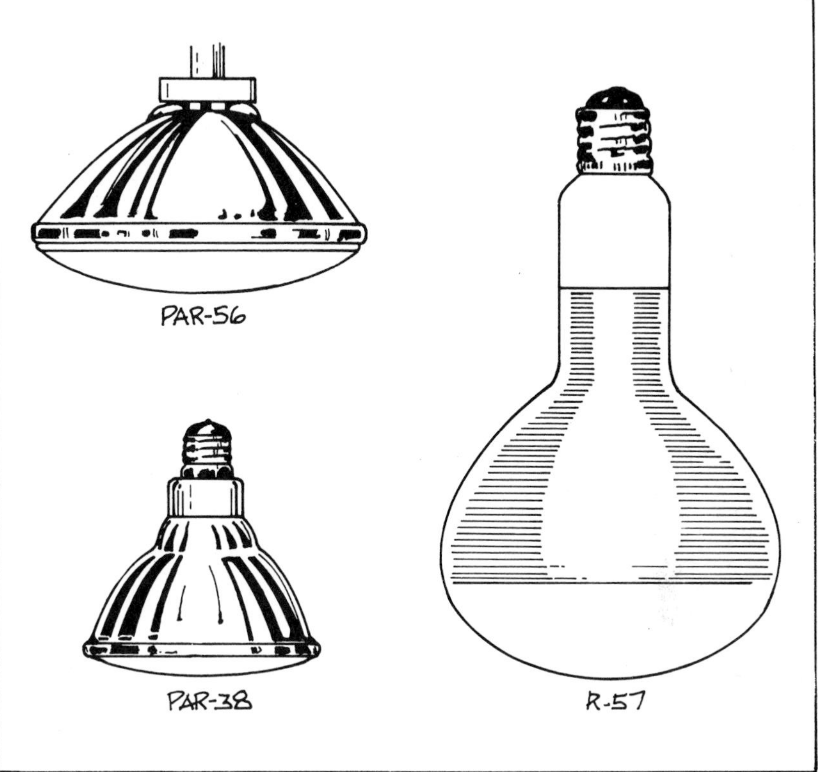

Mercury vapor lamps, above left, are excellent for exterior lighting as they are high-intensity discharge lamps. Light is produced by the passage of an electric current through a vapor or gas rather than through a tungsten wire. Light results from the energy given off as disturbed atoms return to their normal state.

PAR-bulb and R-bulb lamps, above right, combine in one unit a light source and a highly efficient sealed-in reflector consisting of vaporized aluminum or silver applied to the inner surface of the bulb. PAR bulbs are made of hard or heat-resisting glass.

Because of new engineering developments, the sodium lamps deliver 70 percent more light than a comparable mercury lamp, and require 10-14 percent less power to operate. One additional exterior lighting system you may want to consider is the tungsten halogen lamp. It's a compact, powerful incandescent light source with a crisper, brighter light than conventional incandescent lamps.

Pole Light Mounting Guide

The amount of area illuminated by a pole-mounted outdoor light varies depending on the height from ground level. Although the type of light and fixture affects results, the following chart gives the approximate illumination circle for typical outdoor lights.

Mounting height	Diameter light circle
15′	80′
18′	100′
20′	110′
25′	140′
30′	165′
35′	190′

Since many of the PAR and high-intensity discharge fixtures were originally designed for commercial and institutional application, your local hardware or department store probably is not too familiar with these items. You'll have better luck working with a commercial lighting distributor, who has the knowledge and inventory to assist you in designing an efficient security light system tailored to your house.

Although floodlight systems are highly effective in discouraging prowlers, they can be expensive to install, and not every family appreciates their home being lit up each night like a national monument or bank lobby. A low-voltage ground light system, under the guise of landscape lighting, can be less expensive, more attractive, and equally effective in providing household security. Small spotlights or low-level mushroom lights scattered throughout the shrubbery can highlight your landscaping efforts and shed enough illumination along windows and doors to provide an adequate deterrent.

All exterior lighting requires weatherprooof connections, and most is usually covered by local electrical

Spotlights or floodlights can be installed on freestanding poles for outdoor security, as in the photo above left. Consult the fixture manufacturer for information on the proper mounting height to gain maximum illumination from a particular bulb or fixture.

Heritage Lanterns has created an exterior light, above right, whose design is based on an English street lamp from the 1700s. The original models were fueled by oil, but the modern version can accommodate any bulb suited for exterior use.

codes. Ideally, all outdoor lights should be capable of being turned on by the flick of a switch from any of several locations within your house. If you normally arrive home after dark, a photoelectric eye or preset timer can be installed to turn on your security lights at dusk.

Because exterior illumination of your property discourages prowlers and thieves so effectively, the cost of a system is easily offset by the peace of mind you enjoy with a totally secure home.

Doors and windows are the natural entry points for any burglar. A top-quality deadbolt lock and pick-proof cylinder is your best investment, but install it in a solid core, rather than hollow core, exterior door. Windows, with the exception of jalousie models, usually have an adequate inside lock. Jalousie windows, with horizontal adjustable glass louvers, such as venetian blinds, are virtually impossible to protect. If at all possible, replace them with another style window, especially if you live in a high crime area.

Even a stout door or a locked window will not stop a determined, experienced thief. Rather than spend the time and create the noise of forcing entry, he may simply break or cut the surrounding glass, reach inside, and unlock the door or window. In vulnerable locations, it is a good idea to replace standard single-strength glass with plastic or reinforced glass glazing. Refer to Chapter 2, Natural Lighting, for information on acrylic plastics, tempered, and wire-reinforced glass for window use. The cost is nominal compared to the trauma and expense of a break-in. Most security reglazing can be easily handled by a homeowner with average handyman skills.

Interior Lighting for Security

The last thing any professional burglar wants to do is break into an occupied house. The uncertainty and risks are too great. If you can fool the potential prowler into thinking someone is home, then he will bypass your property in favor of an obviously empty house. But it takes more than a single lamp burning in front of the picture window to scare off an experienced intruder.

Several lights in interior rooms may provide better deception, but a system of timers programmed to reconstruct normal household activity with both light and sound is by far

more convincing.

Automatic timers are available in a number of styles, designs, and price ranges. Some models have an extension cord that plugs into an outlet, and then the appliances are connected to the unit while it sits on the floor or tabletop. Others plug directly into an outlet. If you are building or undertaking extensive remodeling, timers can be recessed in the walls and become a part of the house wiring.

When selecting a security timer system, there are several key factors to keep in mind before making a final decision. What type of timing program is the unit capable of handling, and what is the total appliance capacity of the timing unit?

Some inexpensive timers are only programmable for a 12-hour period. These may be sufficient for short term use only—from 6 p.m. to 6 a.m. They obviously provide limited deception for a professional burglar. The standard timers operate on a 24-hour schedule and provide a much more realistic appearance of an occupied home. More expensive models provide an automatic variable timer sequence, which can turn lamps, radios, and TVs on and off at slightly different times daily when you're not home. It's a sure way to confuse any burglar who may have your house under surveillance for several days trying to figure out your living pattern.

Before buying any timers, first determine the number of appliances that will be connected to each and the total amount of power needed to handle your deception program. The last thing you need is to burn out an appliance or the timer because you have overloaded the system. All manufacturers list the capacity of each timing unit.

You can play television or movie director and program your own "average day" scenario, but make it realistic. It might go like this:

6:45 a.m. — bathroom light goes on
7:00 a.m. — kitchen light goes on
7:40 a.m. — kitchen light goes off

At several times during the day, additional lights, radio, TV, and vacuum cleaner can go on and off.

6:05 p.m. — kitchen light goes on
7:20 p.m. — TV goes on
8:10 p.m. — kitchen light goes off
8:45 p.m. — upstairs hall light goes on

This new design in outdoor post lanterns from Progress Lighting, left, will coordinate with a house that's country in feeling. Part of any landscaping plans should be careful placement of outdoor lighting to set the decorating mood, allow outdoor entertaining at night, and provide security.

This 24-hour timer from Micranta, upper right, provides a realistic inhabited appearance to an empty house. Before buying any timer, first determine the number of appliances that will be connected to each and the total amount of power needed to handle your deception program.

Medeco Security Locks announces its new deadbolt lock, lower right. This deadbolt incorporates the inherent features of a high-security cylinder that is widely recognized for its antipicking and drilling properties.

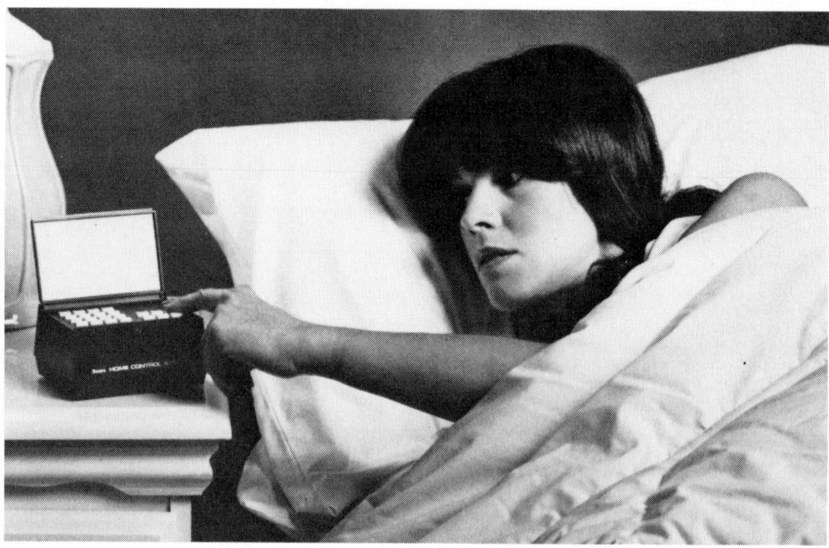

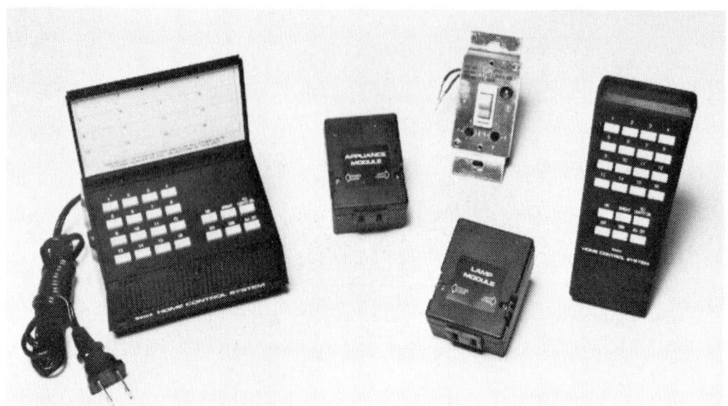

Sears, Roebuck and Co.'s command console, top right, turns on indoor and outdoor lights simultaneously with the touch of a button. It plugs into any electrical outlet near a nightstand or throughout the house. Coded signals are sent over the home electrical wiring system to plug-in lamp, appliance, or wall switch.

Another view of the Sears' Command Console, lower left, shows the remote control unit (right) that can operate the console up to 30 feet away. The light switch module is installed like a light dimmer.

Leviton has designed a new full-range tabletop lamp dimmer, lower right, with slide control, incorporating the latest in reliable solid-state electronic circuitry. Designed with the rich, walnut-grained look of fine furniture, this dimmer plugs directly into any conventional wall outlet.

9:00 p.m. —	one upstairs bedroom light goes on
9:25 p.m. —	second bedroom light goes on; first goes off
10:30 p.m. —	TV off; master bedroom light goes on
11:10 p.m. —	all bedroom lights go off

The trick is to duplicate typical household activities. We don't live on a strict schedule, so avoid reproducing activities on the hour or half hour unless they conform to normal TV scheduling.

To make your programming even more realistic, one company now offers professionally recorded 8-track tapes designed to reproduce normal household sounds. It includes telephone conversations, TV background, appliance sounds, and other daily activities. If you have a tape recorder and a normally active family, you can produce your own program complete with bickering children, barking dogs, and arguments over TV selections.

There is a new remote control timer that may be of interest to some. It operates much like an automatic garage door opener. If you drive up to your house some dark night, you can turn on lights within your house simply by pushing the hand-held switch without leaving the security of your car. This device supplies comforting assurance that no burglar is lurking inside your home.

Home Control Centers

Several distributors, such as Sears and Radio Shack, now offer remote control home center units. These small, relatively inexpensive units are not timers since they cannot be programmed to operate automatically. However, the electronically coded signals from the remote control center allow you to turn on lights and other appliances throughout your home from almost any convenient location.

The center plugs into and operates through your existing house wiring. Appliances are connected to remote modules, which receive the signal from the center. If positioned in your bedroom, you can conveniently start the coffee perking in the kitchen each morning or extinguish a forgotten bathroom light at night without leaving your bed. As a security device, the center can instantly turn on both interior and exterior lights if you should awaken to strange noises around the house.

Photography: The Bottom Line

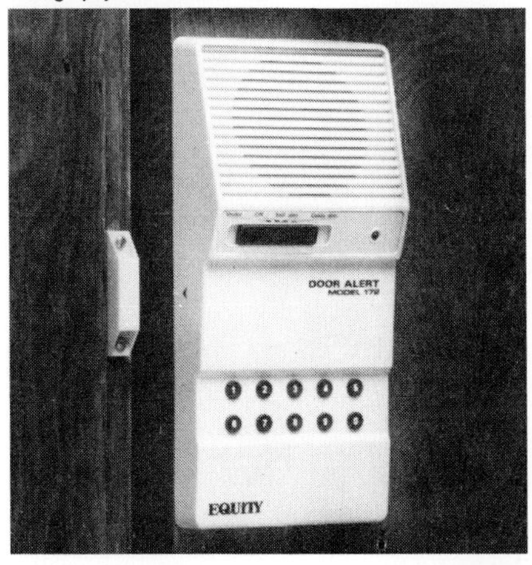

Photography: Detection Systems

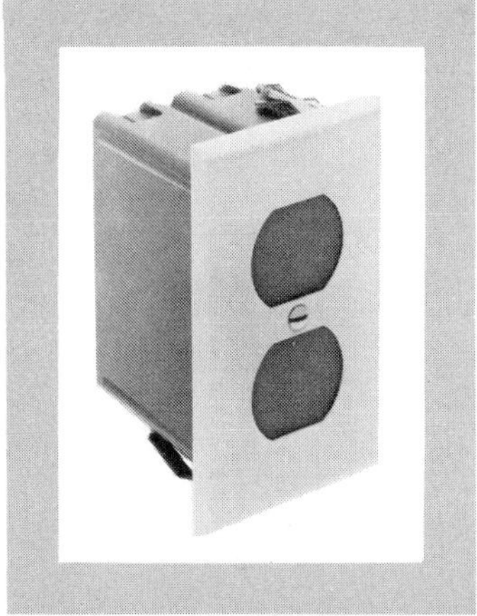

Photography: Sears, Roebuck

Door Alert, upper left, provides continuous protection from forced-door intrusion—whether the occupant is home or away— by sounding a loud, piercing alarm. The unit can only be silenced by the owner's three-digit private code number.

Leviton's dimmer switch, lower left, works extremely well on all incandescent lighting, but should not be connected to fluorescent lights, TV sets, or stereo equipment.

Detective Systems has designed a passive infrared system, upper right, that detects intruders by their body heat. This unit is flush-mounted to resemble an AC outlet and avoid detection.

This home security system, lower right, enables do-it-yourselfers to install their own early warning system against fire and intruders. A receiver picks up radio signals from transmitters hooked up to intrusion switches and smoke detectors throughout the house.

The dimmer feature works fine on all incandescent lighting but should not be connected to fluorescent lights, TV sets, or stereo equipment.

Intruder Alarms

The electronics industry is working overtime to respond to the growing rate of crime statistics. Two basic types of intruder alarms are being produced today:

1. *Trip switches*, including magnetic switches for window and door openings, circuit tapes usually wired to glass areas, and pressure mats that sound an alarm when they are stepped on.

2. *Motion detectors*, which are either ultrasonic detectors set off by the noise of a moving intruder or invisible infrared light detectors triggered when a burglar breaks the unseen light beam.

Most intruder alarms use noise as the protective element in the system, the theory being that wailing sirens or blaring horns will scare off the intruder while alerting you and the neighbors to call the police. Some use a silent alarm wired directly to a security agency or police, or employ an automatic dialing system to call the police. The thinking here is that the silent alarm allows the police to arrive and catch the criminal in the act instead of scaring him off with noise. A few more sophisticated systems combine both noise and silent alarms simultaneously.

The subject of intruder alarms can be a confusing one, and it is too important to you and your family to make a mistake. Both perimeter and interior alarms have advantages and disadvantages. Young children who wander at night or roving household pets can set off false alarms. Even adults find some systems too complicated and forget to switch off alarms as they enter or leave their own houses.

After a series of false alarms, neither the neighbors nor the police will be too anxious to rush to your assistance when the alarm sounds the next time.

A free pamphlet, *Home Security Alarms: What They Are and How They Work*, is published by the National Bureau of Standards. Write to Home Security Alarms, Dept. 676E, Consumer Information Center, Pueblo, CO 81009. For a second brochure, *Home Security Starts At Your Door*, write Consumer Information Center, Dept. 592E, Pueblo, CO 81009.

Designer: Nancy Morrison, ASID
Photography: Harold Davis

An important contribution to interior decoration is the proliferation of house plants. Research shows that plants actually waste a large part of the light they get from the sun. Growing plants in artificial light is easier and more flexible.

11 Light for Plant Growth

Plants, covering everything from fern and cacti to flowers, herbs, and vegetables, add a natural touch to even the most citified homes. Depending on your selection, plants can be decorative or functional, but above all, they represent something alive and growing rather than mechanical and manmade.

Every successful gardener understands that healthy plants need four simple elements—water, air, soil, and light. The first three are relatively easy to control. Plants can be watered on a regular basis either through natural rainfall or by hose, watering can, or mist sprayer. Air, fortunately, is all around us and is free. Any atmospheric condition detrimental to plant growth is also harmful to humans. If you can survive, so can your plants.

Soil may vary according to individual plant needs, but is usually composed of three major ingredients. Sand makes the soil porous so water can drain through it. Clay, which packs together when moist, helps hold the soil together. Humus—leaves, stems, and roots in various stages of decay—adds nutrients for growth and helps the soil retain moisture. Various fertilizers can replenish nutrients as plant growth depletes the original soil mix.

But light, the fourth element, is probably the least understood even by experienced gardeners. Natural sunlight is inconsistent and highly variable. On a bright summer's day, for instance, the direct sun will generate about 10,000 footcandles of light, while a cloudy winter day may only provide between 500 to 2,000 footcandles. Sunlight is not uniform in its intensity nor is it consistent in duration. During the summer, depending on your section of the country, sunlight may be available up to eighteen hours each day. During the winter months, even on a clear day, sunlight may be reduced to seven hours or less.

Even moving your plants indoors to a window sill won't solve all the problems. Many gardeners feel this is a foolproof location with enough sun and warm average room temperatures. Yet a summer sun as it passes through the window glass is often magnified and intensified to the point of being too hot. The concentrated light rays dry out the soil and can even burn delicate plant leaves. During the winter months, the area immediately adjacent to outside windows can be considerably colder than the room interior. Most plants require 50 degrees Fahrenheit or more for good growth. If you are not sure that your plants are in a warm enough area, use a thermometer to check the temperature during extreme weather conditions.

Photosynthesis

Light may be inconsistent and variable, but it is a vital element for successful plant growth. You may recall the word "photosynthesis" from your science classes. It combines two Greek words—photos, meaning light, and synthesis, a putting together. When used in a botanical sense, photosynthesis refers to the process by which green plants manufacture their own food. The plant takes carbon dioxide from the air and water and nutrients from the soil, then, with the energy from the sun or

Photography: Westinghouse

Photography: Joshua Freiwald

This three-dimensional greenhouse window, above, expands a room visually and serves as a display for indoor plants. The plants benefit from the direct sunlight coming through the window. Greenhouse windows can make striking kitchen and dining room extensions.

In the summertime when your fireplace isn't in use, why not turn it into a planter, as in the photo above right. Accent lights from either side provide light and shadow patterns on the white brick background as well as supplementing natural light to help plant growth.

other light source, combines the items to generate plant sugars. These sugars are burned or consumed to create energy for the plant's growth functions. Light is the energizer, the driving force behind growth.

While natural sunlight has been the traditional plant energy source, more and more homeowners and apartment dwellers are moving their gardens indoors where they can be enjoyed all year long. Natural light sources for indoor gardens fall into four major categories:

A. Direct sunlight—coming through a window onto the interior sill. Both east and west exposures provide morning or late afternoon light while windows facing toward the south collect sun and warmth for most of the day.

B. Bright light—can be found in the interior of sunny rooms or reflected from light-colored walls. A north-facing window can supply bright light without direct sunlight.

C. Diffused or filtered light—may come through a transparent curtain or be filtered through trees and shrubs adjacent to the window. Patio and roof overhangs also partially block light transmission.

D. Minimum or low light—refers to room interiors, dark corners, or windowless areas in a home.

While many plants can be grown in sunny or bright locations, few can thrive in filtered and low light areas. However, these minimum light locations are ideal spots to introduce artificial lighting.

Artificial Plant Lighting

Growing plants under artificial lights has been going on for longer than most people realize. As far back as the 1890s, Liberty Hyde Bailey, noted U.S. botanist, horticulturalist, and educator, was using arc lamps for his plant experiments. In addition to his research and transformation of horticulture from a craft to an applied science, Bailey authored sixty-three books and edited four encyclopedic works in the fields of botany, horticulture, and agriculture.

Light gardening, however, did not become popular until after World War II, when mass marketing of fluorescent lights and the discovery of the African Violet (which thrived under them) happened. The combination of inexpensive and available artificial lighting plus a new and attractive plant species encouraged indoor plant growing as a hobby.

Photography: Harold Davis Designer: Virginia Heap, ASID

Decorating with indoor plants requires a green thumb as well as a good eye. Healthy, thriving house plants need adequate light, correct temperatures, proper humidity levels, and the right care. The decorating accents plants provide make them well worth the trouble.

Plant Information and Light Levels

Garden books usually indicate which plants need strong light and which can grow well in low light conditions. Unfortunately, "needs direct light" or "can be grown in north window" aren't very specific light measurements. Use the following *general* guidelines to help translate plant information into light level requirements.

1. Low or northern requirements = 15 to 25 footcandles minimum

2. Medium, average, or east-west window requirements = 25 to 50 footcandles minimum

3. Direct, high, or southern window requirements = 50 to 100 footcandles minimum

Agricultural or plant growth lamps can't be measured accurately with an ordinary light meter. Here, use the distance from the light source to the plant as a general light guide.

1. Low light requirement = 12-16 inches from lamp

2. Medium light requirement = 6-12 inches from lamp

3. High light requirement = 6 inches or less from lamp

Artificial Light Versus Sunlight

Just how good is artificial lighting compared to natural sunlight for plant growth? Depending upon the type of artificial lighting selected, it is usually as good as natural light, and some of the newer lamps, specifically designed for gardening use, provide superior growth characteristics compared to sunlight.

Dr. Richard Corth, senior engineer and photo biologist for Westinghouse Electric, stated, "A popular misconception is that the spectral distribution for the ideal plant lamp should duplicate sunlight. Sunlight, although producing excellent growth, is a very inefficient source, most of the energy being unused and wasted. To grow plants efficiently, the radiation source must provide only that radiant energy that the plant will use."

Most of us are familiar with a rainbow, that natural phenomenon occurring when sunlight filters through a moisture-laden atmosphere during a rain shower. The same effect can be seen when sunlight is directed through a glass prism. The result is that the pure "white" light is broken down and defined into the various colors that make up the

Designer: Nancy Greenberg
Photography: Harold Davis

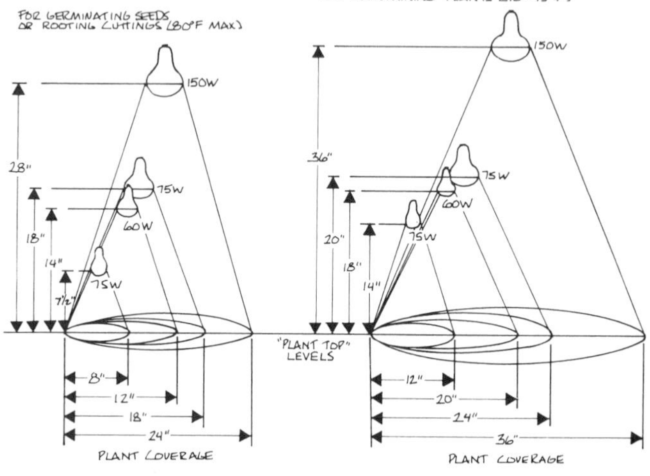

Illustration source: Duro-lite

The hanging terrarium in the photo above provides an interesting focal point above the dining table. Its placement directly underneath the light fixture ensures a proper light source. Clear Plexiglas shows off plants, whether they are resting on it or planted in it.

The diagrams, above right, show the distance at which to place grow lights, depending on the bulb wattage. The size of container is also recommended. You will notice the discrepancy between germinating seeds or root cuttings and maintaining full-grown plants.

spectrum. The color wavelengths appear as red at one end and proceed through a range to blue at the other end of the spectrum with oranges, yellows, and greens in the center bands.

But plants don't need the entire spectrum to grow successfully. The red light waves are used primarily for blossom production, and the blue light is used by the plant for good foliage development. The colors in between—orange through green—aren't necessary for plant growth. Only the end wavelengths, which we see as red and blue, are used.

Ordinary incandescent and fluorescent bulbs supply the full light spectrum, while special plant growth bulbs concentrate on the red-blue colors, which are the best utilized by the plants.

Whether you select regular or special bulbs for your indoor plant garden, artificial lighting can provide some very real homeowner benefits compared to natural lighting.

Flexibility: With artificial lighting plus a little imagination, plants can be grown anywhere in the house or apartment. You aren't restricted to window sills or sunny rooms. Now you can enjoy greenery in all your living spaces. Install plants under cabinets in the kitchen, in bookcases, or room corners. You can create a "farm" in the basement, garage, or attic. Interior room and windowless areas, such as halls and baths, can be brightened with plants. Every square foot of space is a potential garden.

Convenience: Artificial lighting gives you complete control. You are able to forget about seasons, poor weather conditions, birds, and neighborhood children and animals that bedevil the outside gardener. Your artificial indoor environment is safe. Water and fertilize at your convenience. Experiment with new plants at any time of the year. Your biggest bonus is that you can enjoy your gardening activity twenty-four hours a day, every day of the year.

Versatility: Inside, plants can be used to their full decorative potential, as room dividers, to brighten a dull corner, and as living centerpieces on a sideboard or table. The serious gardener can use an artificial light farm in the basement or garage to start plants from seeds or cuttings, which later will be replanted outdoors. Or, he can attempt to grow a new strain of experi-

Designer: Ford Munn, ASID of Noel Birns Interiors
Photography: Harold Davis

Designer: K and G Interiors
Photography: Harold Davis

The potted plant in the picture above left is ideal for its location and is dramatized by a single spotlight located on the ceiling. The plant's container is always a factor to be considered. A container does more than hold the potting mix and house the plant. It also provides decoration. Choose containers that will suit the plant and enhance its decorative appeal.

The plants in this bedroom, above right, are contained in colorful baskets. Baskets can be waterproofed to prevent leaks and water damage, or a saucer can be placed inside the basket to catch runoff. Baskets can be found in a profusion of sizes, shapes, and prices. Natural light for plant growth is regulated by shuttered windows.

mental specie.

Plant lights can double as security lighting when used as a night-light in a child's room, or illumination in a dark hallway or stairwell. And they can act as an antiburglar light when you are absent from home.

For the amateur chef, what could be handier than raising your own fresh herbs and spices at stoveside? You can grow everything from chives, rosemary, and basil to parsley and peppermint. And don't overlook the educational impact of plant life on children. The magic of a buried seed blossoming to life is a wonder to young minds.

Types of Plant Lights

Almost any type of artificial lighting can be used for your indoor garden, but your best choice will depend upon the specie of plant and whether your garden is for grow or for show, or combines both elements.

Regular incandescent bulbs, the standard household variety, can provide supplemental sunshine on cloudy or snowy days or after the sun goes down. Ordinary incandescent bulbs give off light primarily in the red spectrum, promoting flowers and blossoms. In addition, they supply heat, which can be helpful in germinating seeds and cuttings or providing protection to delicate plants on a cold window sill. But because of the heat production, they should be used with caution. Too much concentrated heat can scorch tender leaves and dry out the plant. When using incandescent lighting, place a 60- or 150-watt spotlight several feet away from the plant and check the temperature with a thermometer. Approximately 75 degrees Fahrenheit is ideal, and if temperatures rise above 80 degrees, move the fixture and plant apart to reduce the temperature.

Standard fluorescent lights are classified as daylight, cool white, warm white, and natural. All are heavier to the blue spectrum than incandescent, but they eliminate the heat problem. Daylight has the most blue, cool white and warm white have more red, and natural contains the highest red output. Compared to incandescent lamps, fluorescent tubes are several times more efficient, supplying more light with less energy.

Since neither ordinary incandescent nor fluorescent lights provide a balance of red and blue wavelengths needed by plants, some gardeners

Photography: GTE Sylvania

Photography: GTE Sylvania

Gro-Lux lamps by Sylvania, above, enhance plant growth through the concentration of the red and blue waves of the lighting spectrum. These aid many plants in reaching maturity in a shorter time than if they were raised with sunlight alone. The lightweight unit may be used in any part of the home for improved decor.

Sylvania's Spot-Gro, above right, is a new flexible indoor fixture that can be wall- or ceiling-mounted or placed on any flat surface to accent plants or flowers. The beige and brown fixture is equipped with a cord-mounted switch and may be swiveled in any direction to bathe plants in its blue accent lighting.

combine both types in one setting. A ratio of three watts of fluorescent to one watt of incandescent makes for an ideal plant lighting balance.

Yet many amateur gardeners find this combination of lighting types too confusing. There is a better—but more expensive—answer. Manufacturers have developed a series of special plant growth incandescent or fluorescent bulbs that give the proper red-blue balance in a single bulb. The special agricultural lamps such as General Electric's *Gro and Sho*, Sylvania's *Gro-Lux* and *Spot-Gro*, Westinghouse's *Plant-Gro*, and Duro-Lite's *Vita-Lite* and *Natur-escent* all represent a better plant light balance in a single fixture. These special plant growth lights cost from a third to twice as much as standard incandescent or fluorescent bulbs. However, most serious gardeners consider this a good investment for the ideal conditions they provide and the confusion they eliminate.

Successful Light Gardening

Gardening under artificial lights can be an easy and rewarding experience if you keep these basic suggestions in mind.

1. Select lighting specially balanced for the type plants you want to grow. Choose from incandescent, standard fluorescent, or the newer agricultural lamps designed for plant growth.

2. When using a fluorescent arrangement, select at least a two-tube and reflector unit. Long tubes are more efficient than short ones, and two 40-watt tubes are more economical and efficient than four 20-watt tubes.

3. Where plants receive no natural outside light, most require fourteen to sixteen hours of artificial light daily. Some low light species may need less than twelve hours during the wintertime. Use an automatic light timer for convenience and as a "plant sitter" while away on vacations.

4. Monitor your plants at first. If the leaves turn yellow or the growth is too compact, increase the distance between the plant and lights. Where the plant looks spindly, reaching for the light, or chlorophyll is working overtime producing too green a leaf, move the plant closer to the light.

5. Proper lighting is not the entire answer. Good soil, nutrients, and adequate moisture are all necessary.

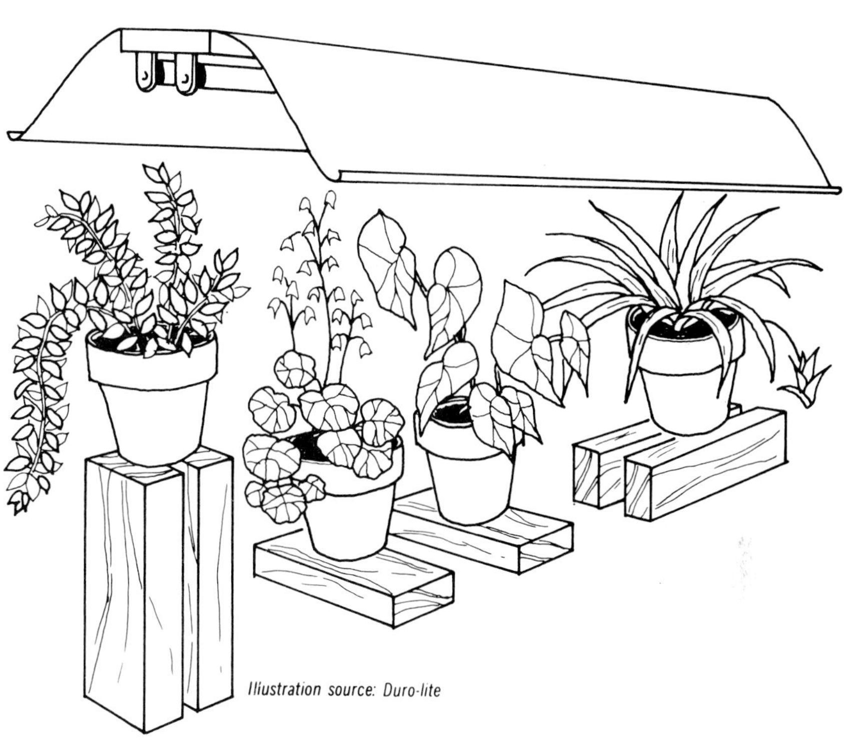

Illustration source: Duro-lite

The Sun Stick by Sylvania, above left, combines ballast and plastic housing in a single unit that can be quickly and easily installed in any indoor location. All you need—pressure tape, mounting tabs, and screws—is included.

The illustration above right shows the easiest way to keep your plants the proper distance from the lights. This is done by raising and lowering them on staging blocks cut from 2x4s. To maximize light reflection and add a striking visual effect, you might paint them white.

Using Plant Light Fixtures

When establishing an indoor garden or greenhouse for your plants, three things must be considered: the quality, quantity, and intensity of your lighting system. The variety of types and sizes of fixtures available today can answer these three points and provide you with a high-styled living room display garden or a working plant farm in the basement.

The quality of light refers to the balance of red and blue wavelengths obtained by ordinary incandescent or fluorescent lights, combinations of both, or use of the specially designed growth lighting.

The quantity or amount of light is equally important. To be most effective, foliage and flowering plants should be placed 6 to 12 inches away from lighting, and succulents and cactus about 6 inches away. As you move plants away from the light source, the amount of effective light falls off rapidly. For instance, the light intensity 6 inches directly below a 40-watt fluorescent fixture is approximately double that of 18 inches away. Light intensity also varies along the length of a tube. It is highest in the center and weaker toward both ends. That means that if you are starting seedlings, the fast growers should be placed toward either end of the tube, and the slower growing varieties in the center.

Intensity refers to the duration plants are exposed to artificial lighting. Experts recommend that light timers be installed with your indoor garden to control day length. Plants, like humans, need occasional rest periods. With automatic light timers you can easily establish day and night or winter and summer hours for your plants. An artificial winter may be a 10-hour day, while summer may require an 18-hour day.

Horticultural books and information supplied by plant manufacturers will help you work out the proper growing/resting sequence for various plants.

The physical arrangement of your indoor garden depends on the type of plants and your personal decorating tastes. Incandescent fixtures can be mounted individually or in sets on ceilings or walls. Installed in track fixtures, either vertically or horizontally, they can be easily positioned for best efficiency and decorative impact. Track installations also provide the flexibility for re-arranging your lighting as plants grow

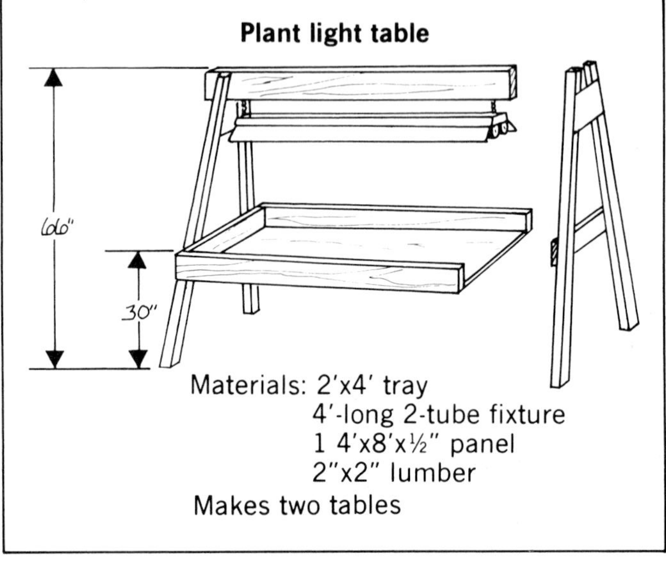

This two-tiered lighted unit, above left, features two 20-watt Westinghouse Agro-Lite lamps. They are housed in adjustable reflectors to give height flexibility. A timer is set for proper growth and foliage maintenance. This makes plant enjoyment year round.

The simple plans above right show how you can make your own plant-light ladder for your home. One 4'x8'x½" panel plus a piece of 2'x2' lumber makes two of these plant-light tables.

or newer, different sized plants are introduced into your garden. Because of the heat generated by incandescent lights, it is advisable to use ceramic sockets rather than Bakelite or cardboard fixtures.

Fluorescent fixtures can be used vertically, either wall-mounted or floor-standing, for tall or vine-growing plants in a corner. This allows uniform lighting along the plant's full length. Used horizontally, fluorescent fixtures are usually suspended above the plants in small countertop gardens or shelves, or built into floor-standing gardens.

Fluorescent plant growth fixtures are available in lengths from 24 to 96 inches, and the longer units are considerably more efficient than the shorter models. Fluorescent lights expire slowly from the ends as they age while the middle section remains the brightest. Since the longer units have more "middle," they retain their effectiveness for a greater time.

Indoor Grower's Light Efficiency

Indoor gardening is not expensive, but you can reduce your costs by considering these suggestions.

1. Maximize your lighting by providing reflective surfaces around your plants. Use light-colored walls, mirrors, reflector shades on fixtures, aluminum foil as reflective mulch over the soil, or white quartz chips in pebble trays and pot tops.

2. Even if they look in good condition, replace fluorescent plant tubes every twelve months. Cleaning the lamps and reflectors every month will also increase efficiency.

3. In the right places, light gardening can serve a dual function. Use it as part of your decorating and safety scheme. A garden in the bathroom, stairwell, or other location can serve as a night-light and makes an effective antiburglar light as well.

4. Where some natural light is available, use your artificial plant lighting on a part-time basis. Afternoon and evening use only will be less expensive, yet allow you to enjoy the look of the plants during the evening hours.

5. Where possible, use your artificial plant lighting on a seasonal basis only. During the summer, move your plants outside, acclimatizing them slowly for the first few days.

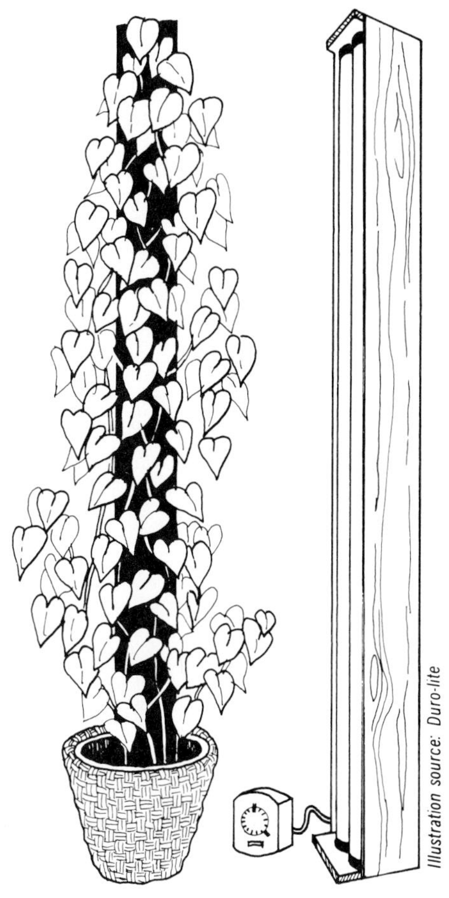

The sketch above left shows how fluorescent tubes placed vertically give tall plants good light from tip to soil level. An automatic timer makes the indoor sunshine self-regulating.

General Electric's Gro and Sho plant light, above right, is just what the doctor ordered for your plants. It gives more light and tender loving care to ensure healthy plant growth. Gro and Sho lights are available in fluorescent tubes, as shown, or in light bulbs.

A number of indoor light gardens, commercially made trays with adjustable light brackets and redwood, plastic, and metal units, are available at local garden centers and hardware stores. Yet many gardeners build their own fixtures tailored to fit their individual plant and space requirements. Simple shelves or garden platforms, with supports for hanging fixtures, can be designed and constructed by the average homeowner with standard building materials. Units can be as fancy or as practical as desired, but, unless saucers are used beneath plant pots, the trays should be constructed of waterproof material. The design should allow lights to be raised or lowered depending on the height of the plants grown beneath.

One building material manufacturer, Louisiana-Pacific Corp., Portland, Oregon, offers a basic A-frame light garden plan with construction details and materials list for 25 cents. The inexpensive garden is designed for use in a basement, garage, or attic. One 4x8-foot panel plus 2x2-inch lumber legs makes a pair of garden trays with adjustable chain-hung fluorescent light fixtures.

To improve your indoor gardening efficiency, provide reflective surfaces around your plants. Reflector shades, light-colored walls, or mirrors will improve the light intensity. Using white quartz chips or aluminum reflective mulch over the soil also improves the lighting efficiency.

Artificial plant lighting opens up a new and controllable world for home and apartment gardeners. Flowers, ferns, cacti, herbs, and even vegetables can now be grown on a year-round basis—all through the magic of artificial plant lighting.

Designer: Ron Fidler
Photography: Idaka

The light fixture in this dining area creates a dramatic mood, but it is also in and of itself dramatic. The modern design and materials of the chandelier are attention-getting, and its setting—the mirrored ceiling and walls—contributes to the total effect.

12 Light for Drama

Previous chapters have discussed principles of lighting, light for decorating and work as well as the practical aspects of illuminating for beauty, health, safety, and security. In almost all instances, the lighting and fixtures are planned to support various activities and complement various surroundings. Successful lighting in a specific area fulfilled a support function without calling attention to itself. This chapter expresses a different approach.

In lighting for drama, lighting becomes the star of the show. It generates its own excitement, creates its own personality, and purposely draws attention to the impact it delivers. Dramatic lighting is not for the bashful or insecure. It's a no-holds-barred approach that makes no apologies to anyone. To come off properly, dramatic lighting must be uninhibited, bold, adventuresome— and it's a lot of fun.

The techniques of dramatic lighting borrow heavily from Hollywood, Broadway, disco-palaces, museums, and a little Barnum and Bailey atmosphere. It draws from display and photography lighting principles to create the desired mood and impact. Properly executed, moods can range from lushly romantic to foot-tapping festive to stark drama. It's a touch of residential show biz.

Dramatic lighting can be surprisingly inexpensive for the punch it delivers. Many of the needed lights and fixtures are standard items. It's the placement, pacing, and unusual application of the standard that makes the dramatic difference. In some cases, special equipment will be required to accent the impact and meld light with color and sound to provide the excitement.

For daytime drama, natural sunlight is a tough source to beat. A well-designed new home or major remodeling project can take advantage of the dramatic possibilities presented by sunlight streaming through windows, patio doors, and overhead skylights. Since the light source "moves" during the course of the day, there is a constant changing and modifying of light intensity and direction as the hours pass. Direct sunlight can be controlled through the use of tinted glass, shades, and venetian blinds to modify natural light. Carefully placed mirrors within rooms will multiply the light level and provide additional decorating opportunities. Sunlight is warm, color correct, and, best of all, free. Used creatively, it can add a dramatic dash to room interiors.

Artificial lighting may use standard equipment as a source, but for impact, pacing and placement are important. Pacing refers to varying light levels within a room for visual interest. High levels of uniform general lighting are safe and efficient and stimulate people to activity. Low uniform levels create relaxation and intimacy. Yet uniform lighting, high or low, can be boring. Where everything is lighted to the same intensity, all objects in a room have equal importance. Without any accents or pacing, the atmosphere is dull.

Light pacing allows you to direct the viewer's eye toward certain objects and away from others. Light intensity tells the eye what you consider important in a room. The simplest and least expensive method

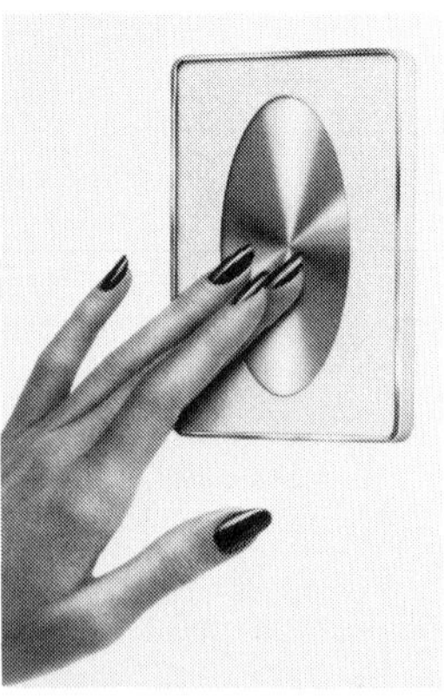

The track lighting by Halo Lighting, above left, brings to life the brilliantly colored wall hanging and highlights the other works of art and the conversation area of this living room. The L-shaped ceiling track features the new Vienti lampholders, which lend a decorative, distinctive note.

Leviton's Sensitron, top right, is a touch-control dimmer that turns on and off and sweeps through full-range dimming. It has a built-in memory that recalls the most recently set brightness level next time it's turned on — all with the touch of a finger.

Lighting mounted on the floor and aimed up a wall or positioned behind furniture can create a very appealing and dramatically different effect, as seen in the photo lower right. Interesting shadows are created when the light from one uplight, a wallwasher, and a high intensity lamp is reflected off the various surfaces.

to establish light pacing is with three-way switches and bulbs. These are not too subtle, but at least you can highlight various items with a low, medium, or high light intensity. Wall-mounted or individual appliance dimmers can achieve the same results with more full-range intensity control. For ideal dramatic control, dimmer systems are usually combined with individual light fixtures installed to create a special effect. Placement of these fixtures often becomes more crucial than light intensity when you are striving for dramatic impact.

Fixture placement depends on the type of fixture and the dramatic job you want to accomplish. Sometimes it is as simple as suspending a bulb and shade from the ceiling to cast a small pool of light over an end table or plant grouping at the side of a couch. The fixture must be hung low enough to avoid any uncomfortable glare for people seated. The fixture may be wired to a ceiling-mounted electrical box or simply hung, swag-style, from a ceiling hook and wired to a wall base outlet.

For dramatic effect, lighting can be mounted on the floor and aimed up the wall behind furniture and plant groupings to create exciting shadow patterns on the vertical surface. The process can be reversed by placing your lighting on top of the walls by installing recessed or surface-mounted ceiling lights. Soffit or channel lighting can be installed to illuminate the ceiling line, directed down the wall or to both areas.

Wall-mounted fixtures, often called "wall washers" for the effect they create, usually cast the light downward, but some open-top models can illuminate in both directions. Track or strip lighting units are increasing in popularity for several reasons. They are efficient, decorative, and flexible. New designs permit a variety of bulb sizes and styles for spotlight and floodlight applications. Reflectors and diffusers make the light easy to direct and control without the hazard of unwanted glare. A track is usually mounted on the ceiling or horizontally on the upper walls, but some interesting effects can be achieved when placed vertically on a wall surface. Here, however, you need to be particularly careful to avoid glare.

Track lighting can be built into new construction, but part of its growing popularity is the fact that most can

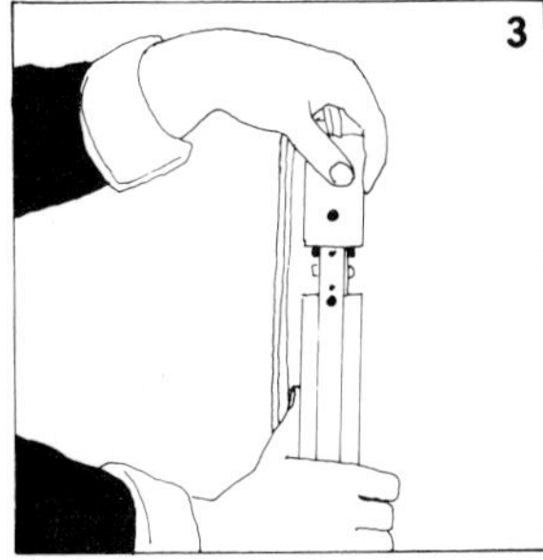

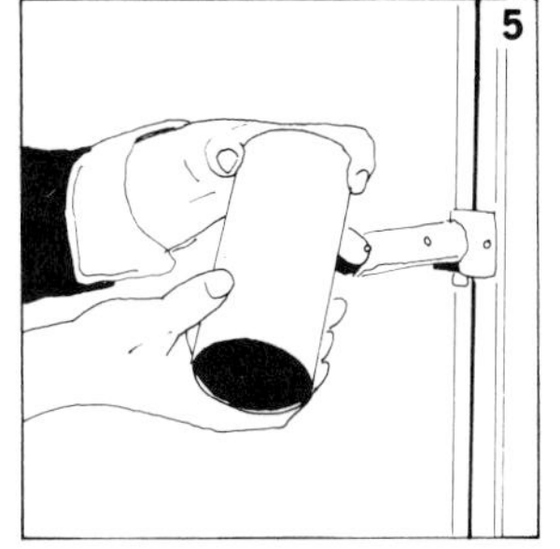

A track lighting system, shown being installed above left, consists of an electrified track of any length mounted on a ceiling or wall with lampholders attached to any point and pivoted to direct the light where desired. Lampholders come in such shapes as spheres, cylinders, or tubes. You can arrange them in "X" shapes, "L" shapes, or in any other pattern you choose. No electrical wiring is necessary because the adaptor makes the electrical connection automatically as it snaps on to the track. Recommendations for placement are 2 to 2½ feet from the wall in a room with an 8-foot ceiling. To install track lighting, follow these simple steps:

1. **Place the track against the wall or ceiling and mark for the mounting holes.**
2. **Drill the holes.**
3. **Insert the cord and plug connector.**
4. **Fasten the track.**
5. **Insert the lampholder.**

George Kovacs Lighting has introduced a series of sleek, modern light fixtures, above right. The clip-on, freestanding style is similar to a photographer's equipment. A lightweight, triangular base supports a telescoping standard for various heights.

be easily mounted in an existing home. Flexibility is the track system's most salable feature. Standard track will accept a variety of size and type of fixtures, and they may be positioned anywhere along the track length. Since no interior decorating scheme is designed for perpetual use, when your tastes change, furniture is added or repositioned, or your lifestyle is modified, the track lighting can be altered easily to meet your new situation. New fixtures can be purchased for the existing track, light units repositioned for new focus, and the system expanded to shed light into new areas.

Where permanent installation of new light fixtures in an existing home presents expensive rewiring problems, consider the use of freestanding portable desk and floor lamps. Newer models have a weighted base for stability, telescoping standards for height flexibility, and swivel shades for directional lighting. Another design series includes clip-on fixtures and freestanding lamps similar to a photographer's lighting. A lightweight, folding, triangular base supports a telescoping standard for various heights. Incandescent or reflector bulbs can be used in the floodlight or spotlight shades.

Candlelight

Although both the lighting technician and the office playboy refer to candle power, they are referring to different effects. There are few light sources that more quickly establish a feeling of warmth, hospitality, or a romantic atmosphere than candlelight. The soft natural glow is most flattering to objects and individuals. Everything looks better—more inviting—by candlelight.

Even when unlit, the graceful shape of tapered or spiral candles in soft colors supplies a visually pleasing arrangement. Candles have the ability to conform to any decorating scheme when paired with the proper style holders. Traditional gold or silver holders bespeak opulence and formality while pewter, copper, and brass designs are found in all styles.

Scented candles intrigue the nose as well as the eye. Popular pine, bayberry, and lilac scents are now competing with more exotic fragrances such as cinnamon, jasmine, spice, ambrosia, and even blueberry. Floating candles can be particularly effective in a floral centerpiece for

Designers: *Tom Quaggin, Tom Hadley*
Photography: *Harold Davis*

This modern dining area, above left, is given a cheery, old-fashioned glow by the extensive use of candlelight. The candle-powered "chandelier" requires long fireplace matches or tapers to light its candles, but the effect is worth the trouble. The glass dishes at the base of the candles catch the drips.

A gentle splash of light provided by General Electric's new Hi-Light, above right, will bring this painting to life. The handsome fluorescent fixture has many decorative as well as functional uses around the apartment or home.

holiday tablesettings. For more informal use, decorator candles, designed to drip a single- or multi-color layer of wax on a wine bottle, help create a Bohemian atmosphere for any partyroom.

Much of the same basic warmth and charm provided by candles can be captured for dramatic interiors when you use decorative oil lanterns. Originally, animal fat or kerosene was used as fuel, but newer, odorless and smokeless oils now available give the same soft glow without the unpleasant side effects. Brass or copper holders with glass chimneys in various styles reflect the flickering light. Oil lamps may be used on the mantel, as table pieces or wall-mounted in sconce fixtures.

Selecting Candles

The two basic types of candles are *tapers*, slender and shaped, and thicker *columns* or *pillars*.

☐ Very tall, very thin tapers (24-30 inches) can be used individually or in groups. They provide above-eye, general lighting for dinners or banquets.

☐ Very short tapers (3-6 inches) are used in random arrangements or combined with tall, thin tapers to cast light on table food.

☐ Intermediate tapers (9-15 inches) are used in a candelabra and sconces. They are available in a great variety of heights and colors.

☐ Flower thins (15, 18, 24 inches in height, ¼ inch in diameter) are used individually or in groups. The most dripless of all candles, they can be safely burned at an angle.

☐ Pillar candles (2-6 inches in diameter, up to 12 inches in height) are larger, freestanding candles that may be used individually or in groups.

☐ Specialty candles include lantern candles, floating candles, decorator candles designed to drip wax, and scented candles either for a pleasant odor or insect repellant use.

Display Lighting

Display lighting is designed to showcase a single object or a number of similar pieces for maximum dramatic impact. The most effective manner for lighting an important picture or piece of sculpture will usually require a little trial and error

Illustration source: Progress Lighting

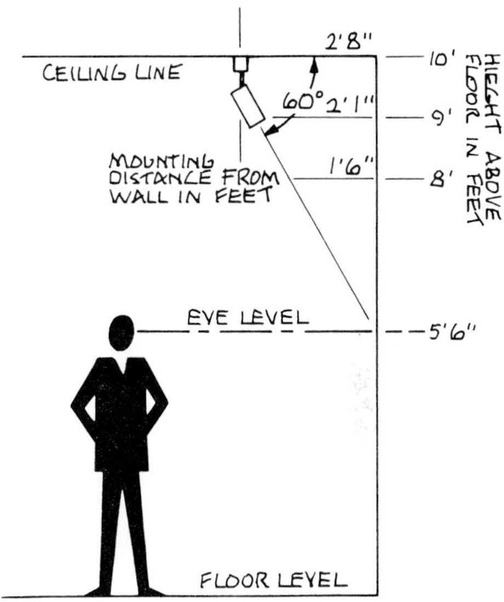

Display lighting such as this track lighting, above left, is designed to show off the painting and antique clock in this living room. Artwork should usually be lighted from above at an angle of approximately 30 degrees from the vertical plane.

The ceiling position for track lighting is shown in this illustration, above right. It is a guide for mounting the track to vertical surfaces. It's based on the average 5'6" eye level. For an 8-foot ceiling, the track should be mounted 1'6" from the wall.

experimentation. Position the object where it is displayed to best advantage in your room and, using one or several portable clip-on lights, try lighting from several angles. Then experiment with several types of bulbs to determine if warm or cool light supplies the truest color rendition of what the artist attempted to convey.

Oil paintings, watercolors, sketches, and prints theoretically should be lighted from above at an angle of approximately 30 degrees from the vertical plane. This is not always possible or ideal in all situations. Start experimenting with your light or lights in this general angle and observe any reflection from oil or shiny surfaces, or light bouncing from glass coverings. Try several arrangements, up and down, side to side, until you work out the best plan. Try to keep the light as close as possible to the picture so that viewers will not be able to stand between the light source and the painting, casting a shadow on the art work. In your lighting experimentation, check to see that your light positions will not directly shine into the eyes of people seated or standing about the room.

Individual pictures or prints are ideally lighted by a special "pin-hole" or "framing" spotlight, recessed in the ceiling 36-42 inches from the wall. These units, with lens and shutters, adjust so that light conforms exactly to the shape of the picture. Surface-mounted single fixtures on the ceiling or upper wall may be used to supply area lighting. For an over-the-mantel picture or even to accent the architectural lines of a carved wood or marble fireplace front, consider installing uplighting at the floor or mantel top.

Where extensive rewiring is impractical, picture lights mounted on the frame top can be used. These should be one-third to one-half the width of the picture, and have a rotating reflector and adjustable extension arm for use on extra-thick picture frames. Tubular 25- or 40-watt bulbs are the most popular.

Picture walls with a number of paintings or prints are usually too difficult or expensive to supply individual illumination for each piece. Here, recessed wall washers, track lighting with adjustable reflector bulbs, or specially designed surface-mounted strip fixtures with lens plates for control of light direction are installed 24 inches from the wall.

Photography: Hibriten Furniture.

Photography: General Electric

Contemporary shelf lighting, upper left, is one of the many innovative lighting techniques used by Montgomery Ward in the decoration of a brownstone. The unobtrusive shelf light featured in the library bookcase provides the proper focus for displaying treasures without disrupting the aesthetic arrangement.

The exquisite artifacts displayed here, lower left, need the interplay of light and shadow to capture their three-dimensional qualities. Track lighting is not the only way to achieve these results. Back-lighting or side and floor lights are also possibilities.

Proper lighting for collection displays, such as the cabinet above right, requires a special approach. These ceramic pieces, being three dimensional, benefit best from the small lights wired to the backs of the shelves to make the objets d'art stand out.

Textural hangings such as weavings, rugs, and tapestries are best accented with shallow angle side lights to show off their three-dimensional surfaces to best advantage. Experiment with floor or wall lights to determine the most effective and pleasing combinations.

Carvings and sculpture need the interplay of light and shadow to capture their three-dimensional qualities. Try backlighting, angled overhead downlighting, or side and floor lights to determine the most effective balance between primary illumination and accent lights to create dimensional shadows. It may take several tries, but the resultant drama is well worth the time.

Proper lighting for hobby and collection displays requires a special approach. Relatively flat items—stamps, pressed flowers, or butterfly collections—can be mounted, framed, hung, and illuminated like pictures. Three-dimensional objects—model cars, ceramic animals, or antique toy soldiers—are usually displayed on open shelves or behind glass in a cabinet or case. Inconspicuous small lights can be wired to the shelf above to shine on objects below. A more dramatic approach is to use translucent shelving of glass or plastic, lighted from below.

Fish tanks provide an exciting display opportunity. Some are back-lit or illuminated from above, but the most spectacular treatment uses blacklight to pick up and highlight the iridescent colors found in some species of tropical fish.

For the serious collector, custom-made display cases are a natural part of their hobby involvement. Wall and floor cabinets, or a coffee table light box (to display an antique key collection) back-lit from below, through a white translucent plastic backing, provide light, furniture, and a point of interest to any room.

Graphic designer, Joe Erceg, of Portland, Oregon, has found a self-illuminating hobby. He collects old neon signs, and presently has 20 or 30 scattered tastefully throughout his home. Most are small commercial signs salvaged when a company went out of business, some are reclaimed from the back room of a sign shop, and a few have been discovered by friends. Unless badly damaged, they were repaired with new tubing and gas for a reasonable price.

If you can collect old neon signs,

Designer: Catherine Armstrong
Photography: Harold Davis

Neon art is one of the most exciting developments in modern sculpture, and it's possible to create the same look in your home. The Joe Ercegs, of Portland, Oregon, above left, collect old neon signs from shops that have gone out of business. New tubing and gas for repairs is all they needed for truly distinctive decorating.

This lavish entryway, above right, makes full use of lighting as a part of the fountains themselves and as illumination of the general scene. The interplay between the lights and the sparkling, cascading water in the fountains is particularly effective. Also, the three-dimensional aspect of the figures is emphasized.

why can't you create new ones? A neon arrow piercing a neon heart with an appropriate set of initials would be a perfect Valentine's Day gift for the right person. Or, if you are on good terms with the cook, the traditional neon road sign, "EAT HERE—GET GAS" might be perfect for that blank wall in the kitchen.

Exterior Drama

Several earlier chapters have covered exterior lighting for safety and security. But in this section we are concerned with a third "S," lighting for *show*. A careful inspection of the exterior of your house and grounds will uncover a number of dramatic lighting opportunities.

One thing you should *not* attempt to do with your exterior lighting is duplicate natural daylight. Avoid the flat, even lighting in favor of combining spotlights and floodlights to develop highlights and shadows that enhance your home's architecture and landscaping.

Landscape display lighting allows you to enjoy your outdoor decorations year round. In the summer, you can view the scenery after dark, and during the winter from indoors, you can see rain or snow falling through shafts of light, creating fascinating patterns. A blanket of snow or ice-covered shrubs take on a special, magical beauty.

Best results can be obtained through the use of a number of fixtures—perhaps several floodlights or PAR lights mounted in trees to shine down and through the branches. Ground-level lights, usually a low-voltage system, can be 8-24 inches off the ground or recessed directly into the earth in flower beds, behind shrubbery, lining paths and walks, or alongside the house. Angle the lights to attain dramatic results.

Be sure to use approved exterior fixtures for all outdoor effects. Ordinary light bulbs will often shatter if a few drops of rain or snowflakes strike them when hot. PAR 38 bulbs or weatherproof plastic lenses are normally required. Check electrical code requirements to be sure of details on approved fixtures and safe installation practices.

Water reflects light like a mirror. Take full advantage of fountains and pools to capture their jewellike excitement. Tastefully used colored lights can be especially effective in this setting. Swimming pools are a natural location to sit and relax.

Photography: Westinghouse Electric Corp.

The simple but imaginative Christmas decorations shown here utilize only three 100-watt flood lamps and one 60-watt incandescent bulb. The first step in decorating a doorway is to make certain it is adequately lighted. Here the two floodlights highlight the decorations and, at the same time, light the steps for safety's sake.

Lights installed in umbrellas, post lanterns, or floodlights in nearby trees can illuminate the pool's perimeter. Lights can be used *inside* a swimming pool as well. A fixture can be placed underwater beneath the diving board and several more around the pool edge for safe after-dark dips. Locate your lights near water with care. Strict code regulations must be followed for safety, and keep in mind that lights reflecting off water can be annoying if not properly positioned.

For dramatic effectiveness on statuary, topiary, or other landscaping groups, objects should be lighted from more than one direction. Overhead, plus side or ground lighting, will accent the full three-dimensional aspects of the objects. Trial and error before you complete the installation can produce the desired effect.

Festive events, such as Christmas, wedding, and garden parties, offer special, if temporary, lighting opportunities. The soft glow of Japanese lanterns strung from trees, or lines of lights around a patio, create their own magic for any party. Tiki torches or floating candles in a fish pond or swimming pool add both light and excitement to any party. Candles in glass bowls supply a festive touch to patio dining, and scented candles or insect-repellant candles can do double-duty for summer entertaining.

Luminarias, or candles in paper bags, may be used the year round. They are most commonly used at Christmas and for summer lawn parties. The bags may be carefully spaced or randomly placed under shrubbery, on walls, up the steps, or in snowbanks lining walks and drives. The practice is becoming so popular that one company, Candle-lite/Christian, now offers Luminaria Kits with 200 white paper bags and 200 white 5-inch plumber's candles, which burn for 6-8 hours.

Luminaria Decorating

1. Carefully fold down the top of each bag 1 inch, forming a cuff. This gives the bag more support when filled.

2. Pour 2-3 inches of sand into each bag for weight and stability.

3. Place one candle squarely in the center of the sand in each bag. Make sure the candle is standing firm and upright before lighting.

4. For a special touch, white bags

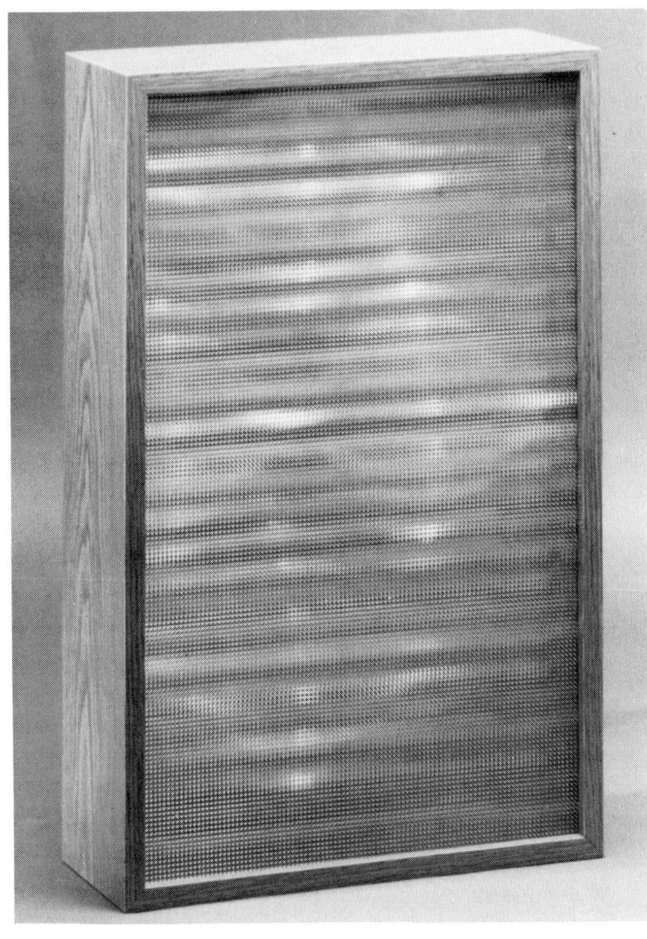

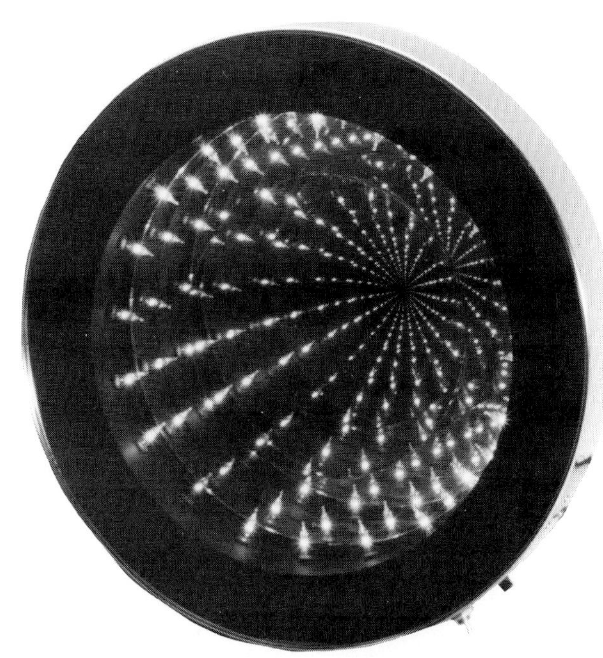

Radio Shack manufactures color organs like the ones above left than can turn an ordinary party into a disco. The built-in sound sensors turn music into flashing colors. They are encased in a stunning walnut vinyl veneer.

These color organs are easy to operated: Plug the unit into any wall outlet, turn line switch to "on," wait five to ten seconds for automatic gain control to cycle, turn down room lights for best effect, and relax and enjoy!

can be decorated by stenciling or felt-tip pens with party theme designs.

5. While the bags are folded flat, use a hole punch to create perforated designs allowing the light to shine through in decorative patterns.

The frantic world of "Disco"may not appeal to your Aunt Maude in Omaha, but if it's part of your scene, you can recreate the flair and flash in your own partyroom. Manufacturers like Radio Shack now supply color organs with built-in sound sensors that translate music into flashing lights—red, green, and blue—that pulsate to the music's beat. Or, to your next party, add a strobe light that seems to "freeze" the dancers in midmotion. Then there is the Psycho light that fits into any standard socket to generate a wild flickering action. The ultimate may be an Infinity light, with its polished chrome mirror and the tunnel of light pulsating to the beat of the music to create the illusion of endless space.

For a less energetic but equally dramatic lighting effect, consider the use of the mysterious "blacklight" and its ability to capture the iridescent and eerie glow given off by some minerals, plants, and seashells. The luminescent phosphors are normally hidden under standard lighting but are visable through the magic of ultraviolet rays.

The special characteristics of some plastics that allow light to be transmitted through it has spawned both decorative and practical applications. Clusters of slender plastic rods, seated in a light base, seem to glow like a perpetual fireworks explosion as they gently wave in a slight breeze. Solid, curved, plastic light fixtures seem to do the impossible when the light rays are bent within the material and used to create a highly modernistic floor or desk lamp.

If light has really taken over your life, then you can put your room into perpetual motion by projecting moving patterns and images onto vertical surfaces. A powerful light can be beamed from a projector or spotlight through rotating wheels of colored lenses or exposed film. Multiple slide projectors can be equipped with timed dissolve units to superimpose a series of images, one over the other, in a seemingly endless parade on your wall.

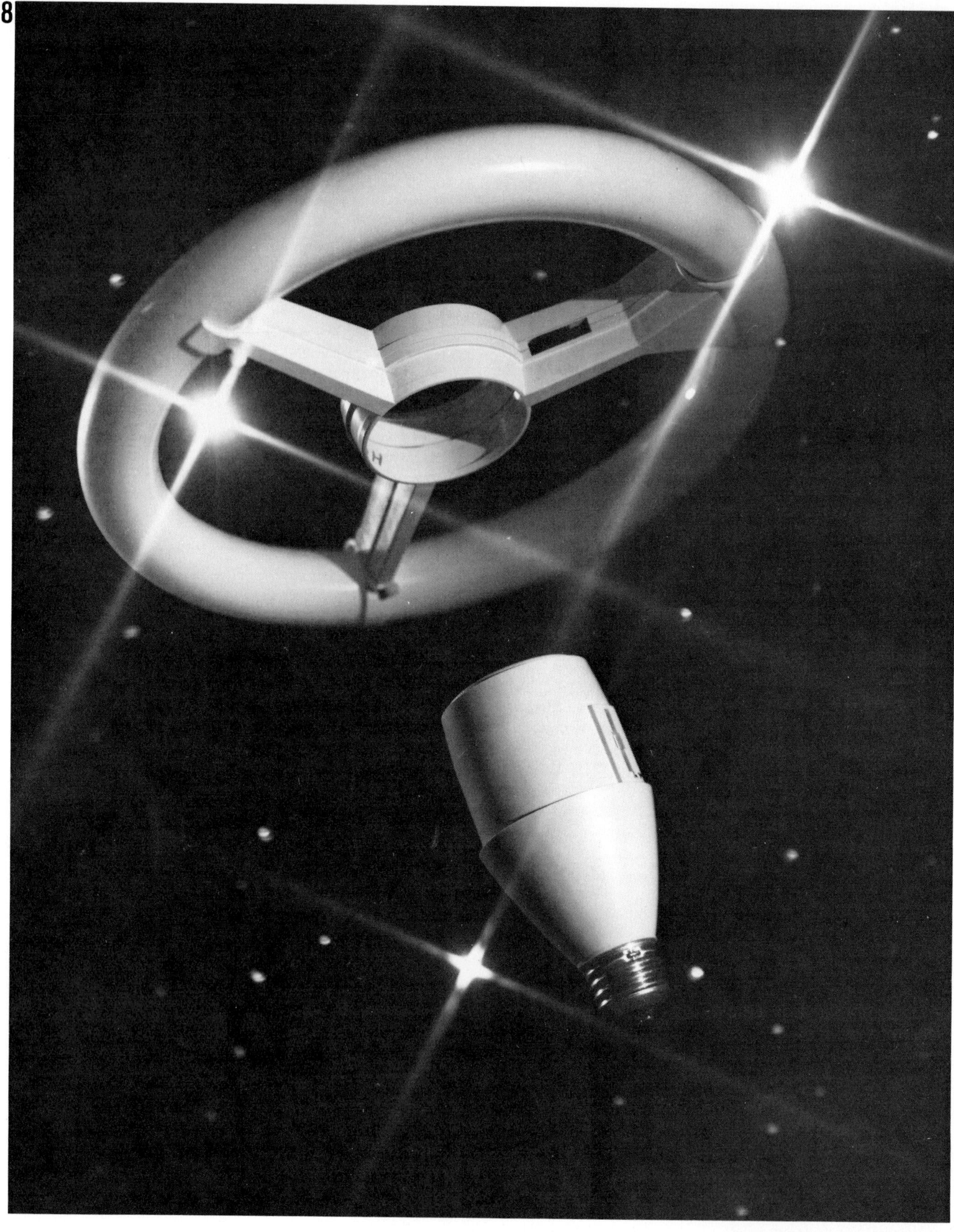

General Electric has introduced a new circular fluorescent light that screws into ordinary incandescent portable lamps or ceiling sockets and more than pays for itself in energy savings. Called Circlite, it uses only 14 watts, yet produces the light of a 100-watt bulb.

13 Light for Tomorrow

Predicting the future is often a risky pastime. Yet, as John Galsworthy stated, "If you do not think about the future, you cannot have one." This final chapter, *Light for Tomorrow*, provides the opportunity to make some fairly safe predictions about residential light and lighting trends in the immediate future and indulge in a little blue-sky, "what if" conjecture for the long term.

The short-term future of residential lighting is fairly comfortable to predict. A number of individual trends, already well underway, will have an immediate impact on housing design and construction and, therefore, on residential lighting.

Briefly, there are a handful of well-established trends that will have a bearing on the light and lighting of tomorrow.

A. *Land*—The growing scarcity and rising cost of land will force a rethinking in housing design. Smaller homes with less square footage but with multipurpose rooms will be the rule rather than the exception.

B. *Energy costs*—Everything that goes into building and operating a comfortable and efficient home will be reexamined. One obvious change will be the increased use of skylights, atriums, and light shafts in housing construction. Our European neighbors who have lived with expensive energy for a number of years have learned to capture this "free" light.

C. *Family formations*—Family sizes are changing from the typical father-mother-several children to more one-individual, working-childless couples, live-togethers, and retired families. There are fewer large families but an increase housing demand for smaller units. The trend is away from rural and suburban living and back to the city for its proximity to educational, social, sports, and cultural activities.

D. *Personal identification*—There is a growing sameness in our jobs, our homes, and our lives. Yet there is a countertrend to this blandness, a growing movement to establish individual identity. Dress barriers in business and social events are breaking down to allow more personal freedom. Creative handcrafts, exotic cookery, and other forms of individual expression are flourishing. Beards and moustaches are sprouting on the young and not so young. Decorative and dramatic use of light can assist the individual in making his personal statement inside and outside his home.

E. *Borrowed technology*—Just as the 1/4-inch power drill and the fluorescent light fixture moved from the industrial production floor into the average home, a host of other proven lights and lighting techniques will find their way from commerical and industrial areas into residential use. The technology is here and the demand is growing.

Some of these lighting changes are being made at an accelerated pace. For the first time architects, designers, and builders are starting their planning with lighting considerations rather than leaving this important element as an afterthought. The space-saving and multiple-use techniques developed by naval architects for ship and submarine design may find their way into smaller residential home planning. As we learn to take better advantage of natural light through

Photography: Joshua Freiwald
Architects: Natkin & Weber, AIA

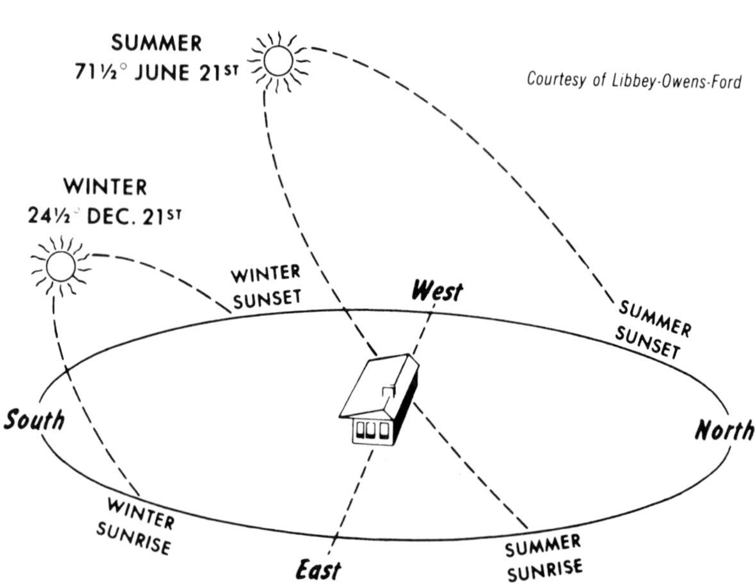

Courtesy of Libbey-Owens-Ford

The home of tomorrow will undoubtedly rely on more glassed-in areas to take advantage of the sun's light and heat. The house above left has a minimum of formalized areas for specific activities, offering the owner spaces of both openness and enclosure. The oak trees surrounding the house let in varying amounts of light, creating changing patterns in the interior spaces.

We are learning to take better advantage of natural light through house placement on building lots. Proper orientation includes careful planning of the house's position in relation to the seasonal positions of the sun as seen above.

house placement on building lots and increased use of glass walls and skylit roofs, today's typical floor plan for a split-level or two-story home may be turned upside down. We may do our cooking, entertaining, and living on the upper floors to take advantage of the "free" light, while we use the lower floor or basement for sleeping and storage.

When you start your planning with light in mind, a number of original and practical ideas make a lot of sense. Natural light can provide the efficiency and drama for daytime living, and artificial light can add the individual touch to a 24-hour-a-day lifestyle.

Building for Light

In the past, poorly designed homes and badly specified windows too often became an energy drain. In winter, windows provided a path for cold air to leak into the home and acted as a conductor of heat to the outdoors. In summer, sunlight became an additional load on the air conditioning system. But, as explained in Chapter 2, *Natural Light*, well-planned windows can become an energy asset.

Tomorrow's home or apartment will be situated on the site to take advantage of solar energy and natural light conditions. More, not less, glass will be used in skylights and window walls. Light control will be accomplished through broad roof overhangs and landscaping with deciduous trees to block the hot summer sun yet capture the warming sunlight during winter months. Insulated glazing for skylights and windows will control heat loss while tinted or photochromatic glass, louvers, drapes, and reflectorized shades will provide for hour-by-hour adjustments.

Unlike today's modern office building, tomorrow's home will have operable windows and skylights to take advantage of mild temperatures and breezes to provide natural conditioning of indoor air. Mechanical climate control systems will feature germicidal and ozone lamps to cleanse, purify, and freshen air as it flows through the system.

On the exterior, safety and security lighting will be built into the original home rather than added on at a later date. Decorative exterior landscape lighting packages will be offered as an option at time of construction. Particular attention will be paid to proper lighting for decks, patios, and

Bronze glass opens up this condominium, above left, to spectacular views while minimizing glare and brightness. The specially tinted glass from Libbey-Owens-Ford has a relatively high heat-absorbing factor that reduces solar heat transmittance, lowering air-conditioning costs.

The residence above right was designed to take advantage of the principle of using solar energy to its best advantage. A long wall featuring Libbey-Owens-Ford's Thermopane insulating glass in window areas permits solar heat to enter the home in winter. In summer, a long roof overhang shields heat rays.

enclosed atrium areas. Here, ground and overhead illumination, infrared heat lamps built into the soffits, and bug lights, either repellant or electric killer, will be part of the standard package. With the growing importance of outdoor family and entertainment activities, the smart builder will capitalize on the sales advantage offered by a well-designed patio program.

As far as lighting is concerned, the most dramatic changes will occur within the home. With today's newer building materials and improved construction techniques, it is quite possible that the home of the future will be a shell of walls and roof with an open, free-span interior. As children arrive, mature, and leave, the family can rearrange interior partitions and walls to suit the changing needs. The residential space will resemble a typical office floor in a high-rise building of today.

There will be less fixed lighting and more portable, directional, and accent lighting available. To accommodate this need for greater interior flexibility, ceilings, the upper portions of walls, and possibly the vertical corner sections will be laced with a network of electrified track channels. Lighting fixtures of various sizes and designs may be positioned anywhere they are needed on the horizontal and vertical surfaces. Modular luminous ceiling panels can be dropped into place for decorative or task lighting functions.

For even more options, the floor may have a power-communications grid system beneath the carpet so that the homeowner, by cutting a small plug from his floorcovering, can tap into telephone, audio visual, or lighting power anywhere in the room. With this system, extension cords trailing underfoot across the floor may be a thing of the past. More likely, the newer thin power-communications tape, developed specifically for the U.S. Space Program, will be used rather than channels cut into the floor.

Technology uncovered for the Space Program has already supplied a variety of glass and plastic coatings to control direct sunlight, metallic reflectorized fabrics, and the thin tape mentioned above, which replaced bulky cables in the small space craft. NASA officials claim they have a warehouse full of answers seeking problems to be solved. Many of these innovations will surely find

Photography: Harold Davis

The built-in recessed ceiling fixtures in the kitchen above are a sign of things to come. The cabinets below the bar would also benefit greatly from innovative lighting ideas such as automatic illumination when the cabinet doors open. Like the principle of interior lighting in cars, this would give the homeowner instant access to material stored.

their way into tomorrow's housing design and construction. After all, a space craft is nothing more than a living unit divorced from land.

Light Controls

The ability to control and use natural light to its full potential will play an important part in tomorrow's home, but even more vital will be the various systems used to regulate the intensity of artificial lighting. More and more light fixtures will be on dimmers so that you can dial a mood, from subtle to spectacular, in any room. Both rotary and switch dimmers are now available to handle any type and size incandescent bulb.

Because of the energy-saving features and light-output efficiency of the fluorescent tube, their uses in residential settings will grow dramatically. Dimmers for fluorescent fixtures are available today on a limited basis. However, as the tubes become more and more popular, less expensive fluorescent dimmers will be offered.

House control panels will be centralized in several locations throughout the home—perhaps one in the kitchen area and another in the master bedroom. Units are on the market today that control both interior and exterior lighting, smoke, heat, and intruder alarms. The homeowner will be able to monitor various light fixtures and appliances with the flick of a finger—turn off the basement light without trudging, and sound an intruder alarm without leaving the safety of his bedroom.

Light switches themselves will be redesigned for more convenient operation. Rather than fingering a switch or rotating a dimmer dial, pressure plates, activated by the nudge of an elbow will be available for the housewife with an armload of groceries or washing. Three-way bulbs and dimmer switches can be touched at top, middle, or bottom to provide low, medium, high, or any light intensity between.

In traditional New England, the proper Bostonians would burst forth each spring, exactly on May 15th, wearing their summer straw hats. The straw hats would be in evidence throughout the warm season until, as if by unofficial edict, they dis-appeared on September 15th. Like the Bostonian, the homeowner of tomorrow may signal the changing seasons by remodeling the tone and feel of his interior lighting system. For

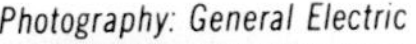
Photography: General Electric

The challenge of an unusual structure, above, has been met by a futuristic lighting system built into the ceiling. Natural light is also tapped with the numerous full-length windows. The decorative arrangements in a room such as this should be made with an eye to the light sources.

those in the temperate climates, cool white bulbs and tubes might be installed during the warmer months to psychologically lower temperatures. During the colder months, the plan would be reversed using warm white or dawn pink lamps. In some cases bulbs and fluorescent tubes would be replaced in the fixtures, but, ideally, rooms might have two separate wiring circuits and twin sets of fixtures built in so that seasonal changes could be accomplished with the flick of a switch.

Some interior and exterior lighting will be tied into electric eyes so that as the day turns cloudy or the sun sets, lights will automatically come on. Times can be programmed to extinguish certain lights as the family retires, other security lighting may burn all night to be automatically shut off at dawn. For both convenience and security, your automobile will be equipped with a remote control switch that will illuminate porch and interior lights when you enter the driveway and before you leave the safety of your car. If you can automatically raise a garage door today, turning on a few lights by remote control will be no problem for tomorrow.

Built-in Lighting

In addition to the flexible light placement systems, the future home may have more built-in lighting for general illumination and for specific tasks—recessed ceiling spots, cove and valance lights, indirect, soffit, and room perimeter illumination. Bath, laundry, and pet areas may come with germicidal lamps in place.

Closet lights will go on when the door is opened. Fireplace mantels will be lit from within to cast light upward, highlighting the architectural detailing of the millwork on the chimney breast. Entrance and patio doors may be keyed to an electric eye to open and close automatically like today's supermarket doors when a homemaker is loaded with groceries or a tray of refreshments for outdoor entertaining.

Kitchen cabinets may light when the door is opened, or the countertops themselves may be an illuminated work surface. Infrared heat lamps will warm plates of food ready for serving without heating up the air in a summer kitchen.

Furniture designers may incorporate lighting into their products. It might be as simple as an illuminated music rack on a piano or

Photography: Ventarama

The ultramodern lamps in the room scene above left blend well with the rest of the decor. The lighting of tomorrow will include freestanding fixtures that reflect the new trends in decorating as well as being technologically advanced.

Skylights, such as the one above right, will become the rule rather than the exception in tomorrow's homes. Motorized, insulated, and double-dome skylights are just some of the refinements that are making this type of window so popular.

as sophisticated as flexible optical fiber plastic reading lamps built into a bed headboard. High-backed wing chairs may have integral reading lights; end and coffee tables will be lit from within to accent items on their surfaces. If not illuminated, furniture may be prewired to accept portable lights and other appliances without the need for lengthy extension cords. If your dining room table featured a lighted surface, picture the dramatic effect of light shining upward through crystal and translucent plastic plates and goblets. It could be even more spectacular with colored or moving lights.

Tomorrow's Decorating

Light will become a feature player rather than take a supporting role in the decorating of tomorrow. It provides the most creative, flexible, and economical method to individualize your environment. The chapters on decorating with light and using light for drama only hint at the many possibilities.

To make your decorating task easier, all paint, wallpaper, and fabric stores will be equipped with comparative light boxes so that you can examine samples in the daylight and under the identical artificial lighting system found in your home. This simple measure should go a long way toward eliminating the disappointment of colors and patterns that look right in the store but somehow are slightly "off" in your living room.

Skylights, greenhouses, atriums, and the use of plant growth lights will allow living greenery for all rooms year round to be a major part of your decorating scheme. Live plants overcome the sterility of modern society humanizing and expressing your individuality.

Light Tools

On a more practical note, light will play a bigger part in some ordinary and not-so-ordinary tools. Today, many shop power tools already have lighting built into their housing—band saws, drill presses, grinders. Hand tools, like the sabre saw, router, and portable drill, are illuminated. There is even a battery-lit screwdriver on the market today.

The working light of tomorrow may well be the laser (Light Amplification by Stimulated Emission of Radiation). The construction industry is presently

Photography: Karl Riek

The photo above is a perfect example of the kitchen of the future. Rough-textured ceiling boards lend a warm informal feeling to the otherwise ultra-sleek lines and furnishings of the kitchen/dining area. Mounting lights at the higher level give more even light distribution.

using the laser beam in surveying equipment for pinpoint accuracy over long distances. Recently, a new process using laser and xenon flashlamp light pulses—the Buck Rogers' ray gun come to life—cleaned the rust from over 5,000 square feet of steel trusses in a Dallas, Texas, courthouse. Project architects said the cost was only 20 percent as much as the cost of conventional sandblasting cleaning processes. Perhaps this laser/xenon combination will someday be applied to cleaning clothes, washing dishes, grinding metal, or serving as "light ray sandpaper."

The forest products industry has successfully reduced a log to boards of lumber without the waste of a kerf and sawdust associated with conventional sawblades using the laser beam. The kitchen of tomorrow may feature a laser knife with the ability to slice wafer-thin pieces of ham or dissect the holiday turkey with the skill of a surgeon. If dress or shop project patterns were printed in metallic or magnetic inks, applied to fabric or a sheet of plywood, then a laser scissor or laser saw could quickly produce an accurate cutting.

As the major lighting manufacturers develop new products, as present industrial and commercial lighting techniques find their way into residential use, the distributing and retailing methods of lighting equipment will change. According to the editors of *Home Lighting and Accessories*, the business magazine for the lighting industry, one such forerunner of the future lighting store exists today. The Light Bulb Center, located adjacent to a shopping center in Houston, Texas, sells nothing but light bulbs. No appliances, no cords, no plugs—just light bulbs.

Just bulbs, but the secret is that the Center carries everything from odd-size cosmetic mirror bulbs to European bulbs for a candelabra.

This chapter opened with a well-known quote about the future, and perhaps we should close with another. C. S. Lewis said, "The future is something which everyone reaches at the rate of 60 minutes an hour, whatever he does, whoever he is." With that attitude, it is not necessary for the wonders of a future lighting system to reach us. Today's technology supplies more than enough excitement if you take advantage of what is available.

Lighting Equipment

1. Bare Bulb Concept
The bare bulb concept in lighting originated with the light bulb as a complete fixture in itself. The *Globelite* bulb is now available in a wide range of colors and in sizes of 2 to 6 inches in diameter. Duro-Lite Lamps, Inc.

2. Polished Brass and Crystal
Elegance and quality are two reasons to consider the new *Signature 60* line of home lighting. These refined lights offer polished gold brass finishes and a lavish use of crystal. The Feldman Co.

3. Electronic Helper
When you open the door to your house or apartment, the new *Light-O-Matic* electronic helper turns on lights automatically. An electric eye sees people and turns on one or more lights (up to 600 watts). Delay periods can be set from 40 seconds to 10 minutes. Novitas, Inc.

4. Lighting in New Shapes
Wood, glass geometry, chunks of glass, and crystal-like rods are unique themes of four new lines of innovative lighting products. The *Radiance* series shown here is available as chandeliers, wall brackets, and close-to-the ceiling fixtures. Lightolier, Inc.

5. Touch-Sensitive Dimmer
The *Dawn* light dimmer is the first UL-listed touch-sensitive dimmer. By touching the faceplate, you turn lights on or off; by sustained contact, you cycle the device from its dimmest to its brightest setting. Leviton Mfg. Co., Inc.

6. Outdoor Post Lighting
The *Country* style outdoor post lantern design is made of weathered solid brass, is 7½ inches square, and fits a 3-inch post. Matching wall torches are also available. Progress Lighting.

7. Beveled Glass Panels
A sparkling addition to a glass series, *Memories of a Crystal Palace Collection*, features heavy beveled glass panels hand set into antique brass frames. Available in a wide range of shapes and sizes, these fixtures are detailed with fine cutting, creating beveled angular facets. Halo Lighting.

1

2

3

4

5

6

7

8

10

11

12

13

14

8. Heritage Collection
This table lamp features a tasteful mushroom silk pleated shade and a crackle finished base. Crackle finish is one of the industry's most respected finishes. The fishtail shape is an appealing Oriental tradition. Philmar Sandel.

9. Wall-Washing Light
The *Scoop* wall-washing type light subtly brightens walls and comes in today's natural tones, bright white, basic bronze, and old green. It has the added benefit of being economical by using general service "A" lamps. Lightolier, Inc.

10. One Material, Many Uses
Sienna basketweave is the motif of this grouping of accessories. It is highlighted by the gingerjar-shaped lamp base crowned with a white checked, linen, pleated shade. Paul Hanson Co., Inc.

11. Track Lighting
The *Snaptrak* lighting system features white and butcher-block finishes and a thin, smooth-faced track. The track easily snaps together and plugs into a wall outlet. The cylindrical light comes in black with an antique brass finish. Progress Lighting.

12. Early Americana Lighting
The new *Connecticut* wall lamps can be installed in bathrooms, bedrooms, or powder rooms. The set of two lamps has an antique brass finish and delicately etched, frosted glass globes. Miami-Carey Mfg. Co.

13. Wood Trimmed Unit
This 12" x 12" incandescent wood trim recessed square features a solid wood frame and latticework, with a matte white acrylic diffuser. The reflector is hydro-formed and includes ribs to diffuse the light and eliminate hot spots. Guth Lighting.

14. Dome Lights in Cane
A grouping of dome lights in clear-lacquered cane has just been introduced. The cane used for these fixtures is the type customarily used in the most costly cane furniture. The Feldman Co.

Lighting Equipment

1. Country Modern Look
The *Country Modern* model is one of a series of five new chandeliers. The deep toned wood-finished center column has gloss chocolate brown accents. The shades are of pearlescent bronze smoke glass. Halo Lighting Div., McGraw-Edison Co.

2. New Track Lighting
The bell-like form of these new track lighting fixtures was designed to complement all decorating designs. The series uses 75-, 150-, or 200-watt PAR reflector spot or flood lamps. Trakliting, Inc.

3. Contemporary Chandelier
Part of a unique and economical contemporary family of chandeliers, this fixture combines smoke acrylic diffusers with glittering mirrored chrome. Halo Lighting Div., McGraw-Edison Co.

4. Four-Shade Chandelier
This uncommon four-shade chandelier features etched diamond panes and is finished in antique brass. A center downlight highlights table settings. Lightolier.

5. Mirage
The *Mirage* chandelier suggests a sculptural formation with its chunky glass. Cubes of glass are inside-etched for warm, diffused effect. The finish is polished and satin brass. Lightolier.

6. Architectural Squares
A new accent for outdoor lighting can be yours with these topaz architectural squares. They are bronze-finished extruded aluminum enriched by topaz acrylic diffusers. Designed for vertical mounting, the top diffuser is completely enclosed to protect the lamp from weather. Lightcraft of California.

7. Energy-Saving Pendant
This double chain pendant for family rooms is equipped with energy-saving fluorescents. It is crafted in solid oak that has been hand-rubbed to bring out natural wood-graining. Lightcraft of California.

1

2

3

4

5

6

7

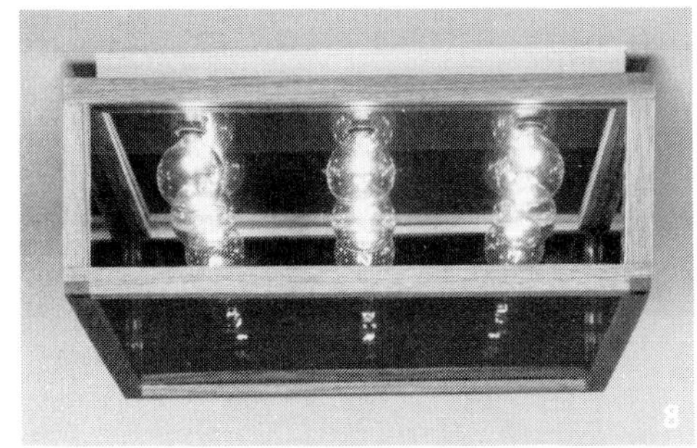

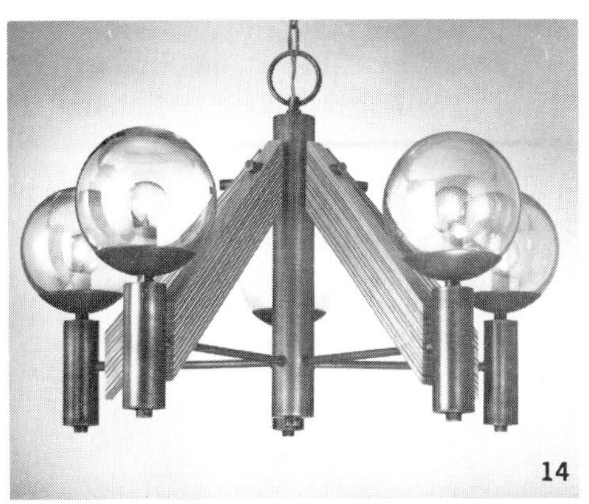

8. Framed Light
Add warmth to your foyers, halls, den, or bedrooms with these bare bulbs that are muted by bronze/smoke acrylic panels. Frames are handcrafted of solid oak, with corner accents of inlaid solid brass. Lightolier.

9. Graceful, Yet Tough
There's a cathedral-like beauty to this handsomely designed outdoor wall bracket. But it's a tough, weather-resistant unit that will help keep you safe and secure while adding a look of quality to your home. Thomas Inds., Inc.

10. Roto-Groove Spheres
These new roto-groove spheres are available for both one- and three-circuit tracks. Evenly stepped black roto-grooves add a distinctive finishing touch to the spheres finished in polished chrome or white. Lightcraft of California.

11. Beveled Glass Pendant
Beveled topaz glass is formed into intriguing patterns and bonded with decorator metal finished in antique brass. The sturdy candelabra base fits eight 60-watt lamps. Lightcraft of California.

12. Pewter and Brass
Pure, simple lines are used to great advantage in this new pewter and brass, six-light chandelier with matching wall bracket. Imported from Europe, the 22-inch-diameter chandelier features gracefully curved pewter arms that sweep up through rings of polished brass to form an open center column. Progress Lighting.

13. Victorian Styling
This low-cost 24-inch diameter, five-light chandelier is an excellent reproduction of Victorian gaslight styling. The gold-banded, etched glass shades have a charming floral design. Progress Lighting.

14. Rustic Appeal
If you love the cozy warmth of a mountain lodge, you'll appreciate the rustic beauty of this contemporary chandelier. It radiates color from five bronze lustre glass globes, natural laminated hardwoods, and a trim in dark antique brass. Thomas Inds., Inc.

Glossary of Terms

A-lamp—the standard light bulb.

Accent lighting—sometimes called sparkle. Light is broken into many bright spots. Typical sources of this type of light are candles, chandeliers, and fixtures with many bulbs. It is also used to describe focusing light to emphasize an object or to draw attention to a particular area.

Baffle—a lighting fixture part that prevents light from traveling in a given direction. It is usually used to shield or conceal a bulb or strip light, for example, from certain angles of view—as above a working surface in a kitchen, or in cornice or cove lighting.

Ballast—discharge bulbs such as fluorescent, mercury-vapor, sodium, etc., try to consume ever-increasing amounts of electric current after having been turned on; if they are allowed to do so, they destroy themselves almost instantly. A ballast prevents this from happening by providing the necessary stabilizing characteristics, usually a high voltage for starting the bulb and a lower voltage for running it. The components that do this are usually packages in a heavy black brick-shaped box with wires coming out from it.

Beam—any fixture or bulb producing a "beam" of light. The beam width or "spread" of the beam is labeled "narrow" (as from a PAR spot bulb), "medium" (as from a PAR flood bulb), or "wide" (as from an R40 flood bulb).

Brightness—when we see brightness, it is actually light coming from a surface—either reflected or transmitted or emitted by a primary source such as the sun or a lamp. For example, a bright coin reflects more light from its surface than a dull one, which has the same area. It is important to define the term and use it correctly because when we talk about brightness in relation to lighting equipment, we usually mean not how much useful light the fixture produces, but how much light comes out from its surfaces and hits you in the eye. When people say things like, "That's a bright light," it is interesting to know whether they mean, "That produces a lot of light" or "That produces a lot of glare."

Bulb—the bulb of the lamp is really the glass or quartz enclosure that protects the filament or other light-giving part. Most people use the term for the whole.

Candle—a standard candle produces 12.57 lumens of light and is still the gentlest and most flattering way of lighting for any number of situations.

Candela—unit of intensity of a light source.

Color—the true nature of our perception of color is still being debated. For our purpose, color is a characteristic not of the surface seen, but of the light coming from it.

Cornice lighting—a light directed downward from the cornice between the wall and ceiling. Lights the wall surface below.

Cove—for lighting, a ledge or shelf on the wall, or a recess in the wall. Cove lighting is upward light thrown from equipment mounted on such a ledge.

Diffuser—a device to redirect or scatter light from a source or translucent material.

Dimmers—device to gradually dim or brighten lights. Meant for lighting only, dimmers shouldn't be connected to other electrical or motor-driven appliances.

Direct glare—offending (excessive) brightness resulting from high fixture luminance or insufficiently shielded light source directly in the normal field of vision.

Direct lighting—light cast directly onto an object, without reflections from other surfaces such as walls or ceilings.

Downlight—a lighting fixture that produces all of its light downward; or light itself directed downward from a lighting fixture.

Fluorescent light—(white light) light produced by the fluorescent bulb, which is tubular shaped and coated on the inside with phosphors. Different phosphors are used to provide different colors. This type of lighting is far more energy-efficient than incandescent and does not give off heat when lit.

Footcandle—unit for measuring illumination.

General lighting—sometimes called ambient lighting. A low level of light throughout an entire area illuminating that area more or less uniformly. It is either direct (light shining on objects to be illuminated) or indirect (light reflecting off a surface, usually the ceiling or a wall). Indirect lighting creates a more subtle effect.

General purpose floodlight (GP)—a weatherproof unit so constructed that the housing forms the reflecting surface. The assembly is enclosed by a cover glass.

Globe—a transparent or diffusing enclosure intended to protect a lamp, to diffuse and redirect its light, or to change the color of the light.

Illumination—technically the level of light (or the number of footcandles) on a surface.

Illumination meter—an instrument for measuring the illumination on a surface. Most such instruments consist of one or more barrier-layer cells connected to a meter calibrated in footcandles.

Incandescent light—(yellow light) light produced by

heating a material, usually tungsten, to a temperature at which it glows. Heat is given off as well as light. Incandescent bulbs accent warm colors.

Indirect lighting—light arriving at a point or surface after reflection from one or more surfaces (usually walls and/or ceilings) that are not part of the lighting fixture.

Intensity—the measure of the amount of lights (lumens) traveling within a beam of light of a given size or spread. It is usually expressed in candlepower or candelas.

Lamp—a generic term for a man-made source of light. By extension, the term is also used to denote sources that radiate in regions of the spectrum adjacent to the visible.

Light—technically, that part of the electromagnetic spectrum to which the eyes respond.

Lighting fixture—apparatus housing light bulbs or lamps. There are five basic kinds of fixtures—recessed, ceiling-mounted, pendant, wall-mounted, and portable (such as a table lamp).

Lumens per watt (L/W)—measure of light source efficiency.

Luminaire—a complete lighting unit consisting of a lamp or lamps together with the parts designed to distribute the light, to position and protect the lamps, and to connect the lamps to the power supply.

Luminous ceiling panels—a type of structural lighting that creates spacious lighting effects. Often sold in prepackaged assemblies for home application.

Mercury lamp—an electric discharge lamp in which the major portion of the radiation is produced by the excitation of mercury atoms.

PAR bulb—(Parabolic Aluminized Reflector) a reflectorized lamp molded out of heavy, heat-resistant glass that is used both indoors and out. PAR lamps are available in both flood and spotlights and are capable of excellent directional light beam control (more so than an R-lamp).

Reflection—in lighting this means changing the direction of a ray of light by bouncing it off a surface. The angle at which it leaves the surface is equal to the angle at which it hits the surface. Most "background" light is reflected light.

Reflector bulbs—(R-lamp) incandescent bulbs coated to direct light where desired. Spotlight bulbs direct their light in a narrow beam. Floodlight bulbs spread their light over a larger area. Reflector lamps direct nearly all of the illumination where it is wanted, making it an extremely efficient bulb.

Soffit lighting—light source housed in the underside of an architectural member.

Structural lighting—light sources built into the home as part of the finished structure.

Supplementary lighting—lighting used to provide an additional quantity and quality of illumination that cannot be readily obtained by a general lighting system. Lighting that supplements the general lighting level, usually for specific work requirements.

Task lighting—lighting providing the illumination for a manual or visual task (sewing, reading) and for the immediate background of the task, but only incidentally, or not at all, for the rest of the space.

Three-way bulbs—bulbs having two filaments. Each can be operated separately or in combination with the other. It is an excellent energy-saver. It can be turned high for reading, writing, or sewing; on the middle setting it can be used for TV viewing, talking, and entertaining; and on the lowest it can be used as a night-light or for a subdued atmosphere. Three-way bulbs are generally available from a 30/70/100-watt size to a 100/200/300 one. You need a special three-way socket and switch to take advantage of the three-way effect. Since there are two filaments in the lamp, there are two contacts in the base. Tightening the lamp in the socket should ensure that both of these contacts are connected.

Track lighting—allowing light to pass through; a pigmented, etched, or frosted surface that is not itself see-through.

Transparent—allowing vision through.

Uniform lighting—when the same quantity of light (measured in footcandles) is provided throughout a given area. The lighting level is based on the maximum requirement.

Uplight—a canister-shaped lighting fixture that produces all its light upward; or, light itself going upward from a fixture.

Valance—a shield or baffle, mounted on a wall well below the ceiling, shielding from view a bulb or lighting fixture installed between it and the wall.

Wallwasher—a lighting fixture that, when installed in correct relationship to a wall, will light it evenly from top to bottom without spilling or wasting light away from the wall into the room.

Watts—in an electrical circuit, the amount of power being delivered as a result of the flow of a current (in amps multiplied by the pressure of that flow of current (in volts).

Manufacturers

Allmilmo Corp.
122 Clinton Rd.
Fairfield, NJ 07006

Brookstone Co.
127 Vose Farm Rd.
Peterborough, NH 03458

Charmglow
Box 127
Bristol, WI 53104

Detection Systems
400 Mason Rd.
Fairport, NY 14450

Duro-Lite Lamps
17-10 Willow St.
Fair Lawn, NJ 07410

The Feldman Co.
612 S. Wall St.
Los Angeles, CA 90014

General Electric Co.
Lamp Marketing Dept.
Nela Park
Cleveland, OH 44112

GTE/Sylvania
70 Empire Dr.
West Seneca, NY 14224

Guth Lighting Div.
General Signal
P.O. Box 7079
2615 Washington Blvd.
St. Louis, MO 63177

Halo Lighting Div.
McGraw-Edison Co.
400 Busse Rd.
Elk Grove Village, IL 60007

Paul Hanson Co., Inc.
Carlstadt, NJ 07072

Heritage Lanterns
Sea Meadows Lane
Cousins Island
Yarmouth, ME 04096

Kohler Co.
Kohler, WI 53044

Leviton Mfg. Co.
59-25 Little Neck Pkwy.
Little Neck, NY 11362

Lightcraft of California
1600 West Slauson Ave.
Los Angeles, CA 90047

Lightolier, Inc.
346 Claremont Ave.
Jersey City, NJ 07305

Miami-Carey Mfg. Co.
203 Garver Rd.
Monroe, OH 45050

NuTone Div.,
Scovill Mfg.
Madison & Red Bank Rds.
Cincinnati, OH 45227

Progress Lighting
Erie Ave. & G St.
Philadelphia, PA 19134

Skymaster Skylights Div.,
Tub-Master Corp.
413 Virginia Dr.
Orlando, FL 32803

Thomas Ind., Inc.
207 E. Broadway
Louisville, KY 40202

Trakliting, Inc.
14625 E. Clark Ave.
City of Industry, CA 91746

Wasco Products
Box 351
Sanford, ME 04073

Western Wood Products Assn.
1500 Yeon Bldg.
Portland, OR 97204

Westinghouse Electric
Lamp Division
One Westinghouse Plaza
Bloomfield, NJ 07003